"Where did the
Justice go?"

Books by Frances Strauss

SO YOU'RE GOING TO GET MARRIED
(*under pseudonym of Bell Wiley*)

COOKBOOK OF LEFTOVERS
(*Bell Wiley*)

NEW WAYS TO BETTER MEETINGS
(*with Bert Strauss*)

MY RHODESIA

"Where did the Justice go?"

The Story of the Giles-Johnson Case

FRANCES STRAUSS

Gambit
INCORPORATED
Boston
1970

Excerpt from "Clemency in Annapolis" by Murray Kempton, *The New Republic*, October 26, 1963. Reprinted by permission of *The New Republic*, © 1963, Harrison-Blaine of New Jersey, Inc.

Excerpts from the *Montgomery County Sentinel*, August 2, 1962 and May 18, 1967. Reprinted by permission of Roger B. Farquhar, Editor.

Excerpt from *Not Guilty* by Jerome and Barbara Frank. Copyright © 1957. Reprinted by permission of Doubleday and Company, Inc.

Excerpt from Draft Statute, *"A State Statute to Liberalize Criminal Discovery,"* 4 *Harvard Journal on Legislation* 107 (1966). Reprinted by permission of the Harvard Student Legislative Research Bureau.

Excerpts from the *Washington Post*, October 31, 1963; May 18, 1964; February 23, 1967; and January 25, 1968. Courtesy the *Washington Post*.

FIRST PRINTING

Author's note

The following names used in this book are fictitious:

William Rogers
Robert Gooding
Stella Mae Watkins, and all other members of the
    Watkins family.
James Fisher
Mark White
John Brooks
Sammy Harper
Prentiss
Dotty Brooks, Mrs. Donald Brooks
Robert Bruce
Tom Brooks
Atkinson
Evelyn Clark
Jane Clemens
Henry Rogers
Mrs. Rodney
Livingston
Hubert McIntyre
Elston Finch
Winterset Street
Genevieve
Walter Biernbaum
Tim Calloway
Arnold Hawkins
Glen Wykoff
Edward Harrison
Arthur Jones
Eliot Jones

Leslie Barons
Richard Johnson
Mrs. Olson
Annabelle Peterson

It seems inevitable that in one instance or another I will have used the name of a real person who has never even heard of the Giles-Johnson case. If so, I apologize.

FRANCES STRAUSS

INTRODUCTION
by Edward P. Morgan

It would be hard to find more devastating proof of the awful fallibility of the American judicial system than the seven-year saga of three young citizens of Maryland. An ugly little incident on a dark night in July, 1961, on a dubious lovers' lane in rural Montgomery County snatched two brothers, James and John Giles, and a friend, Joe Johnson, from anonymity and, in a malignant and terrible miscarriage of legal process, catapulted them all onto Death Row at the state penitentiary in Baltimore. They had been convicted of raping a teen-aged white girl and were condemned to die in the gas chamber. But their real crime against society—as this book will show— was to have been born black. That is another way of saying that the dominating white society of the United States of America in the last third of the twentieth century had, again, itself committed the unpardonable crime of racism.

But though man's continuing inhumanity to man makes a mockery of the term "civilization" in the context of human behavior, in this country and elsewhere, all is not quite lost. The doggedness of the individual human spirit is still a wondrous thing. Tyrants have never been able to extinguish it completely. Its vigor keeps an open society from becoming closed—though, paradoxically, even in modern America the ancient strangling prejudices of race coupled with the suffocating selfishness of our very affluence are putting the spirit of human freedom to the extreme test of endurance.

For the Giles brothers and Joe Johnson are alive and free today, not because of the majestic movement of justice through the courts, but because a stubborn handful of people, goaded by what Quakers call a conscience of concern, pursued injustice right up to the Supreme Court and down again. They won not by following the System but by bucking it at every turn—and nearly every turn was heartbreaking until the last. There was no national celebration of their victory. Indeed, ninety-nine percent or more of the American public undoubtedly are ignorant of the Giles-Johnson case to this day. But they should not be, if this republic is to be saved.

Before that last sentence is dismissed as the desperate hyperbole of an embittered do-gooder, let us ask ourselves, honestly, how much more evidence is it going to take to make us realize where we are headed? How many more Kerner Commission reports need to be published before we grasp the face that we are fragmenting the country into separate, hostile groups forming Apartheid America? How many more life experiences of the Giles and the Johnsons of the land must be told before we concede that the noble motto, "Equal Justice Under Law," carved on the marble front of the Supreme Court building in Washington, is too often mocked in practice? As George Orwell would put it, some people are still more equal than others. We continue to operate on different standards of justice for the rich and the poor, for the Negro and the Caucasian.

Again and again this fact emerges in the record of the Giles-Johnson case. In October, 1963, at a hearing in the state capitol in Annapolis—which finally persuaded Maryland's governor at the time, J. Millard Tawes, to reduce the sentences of the three Negroes to life imprisonment—one of the defense attorneys, Robert Heeney, got to the sociological heart of the issue. "If I could change the color of the skin of one of these defendants," he said, "we would not be before you today."

To a supporting exhibit bearing the signatures of nearly 7,000 Maryland citizens and 1,500 more from the District of Columbia, there was an ironic footnote. This was in the form of a press clipping reporting the fact that on August 28, 1963 —two years after the crime in Montgomery County and on the very day of the huge civil rights march on Washington—a young, white, gentleman tobacco farmer of southern Maryland named William Devereaux Zantzinger had been sentenced to six months in jail and fined $625 for manslaughter. In a drunken rage at a charity ball he had beaten a fifty-one-year-old Negro barmaid with a cane, causing her death.

The sexual element in racism seems to bring out the worst savagery of prejudice. Perhaps we have passed the time when a black man can be convicted of molesting a white woman by simply casting a glance in her direction. But when a Negro is suspected of the craven but titillating crime of rape, he is automatically presumed guilty unless and until he can prove his innocence. In the past this has been well-nigh impossible because the whole machinery of society was geared against the accused. And, as it was put by one of the dedicated attorneys who donated countless man-hours to the defense without fee, Joe Forer, "Innocence is a relatively irrelevant factor of American law."

And, in commenting on the turgid, tortured Supreme Court ruling which eventually, by the most circuitous and frustrating of routes, led to the freeing of the Giles boys and then Joe Johnson, Forer added: "The Court gets cases every day of terrible injustice which they don't attempt to review on the valid grounds that they can't correct all the injustices." But Forer tried to revive the spirits of the exhausted, puzzled, and forlorn defense committee by explaining that though they had neither won nor lost that round, " . . . I think that very inability of the Justices to decide this case indicates that the committee has made a dent on the public conscience. . . . It [the case] was disturbing [to the Court] because it was an injustice the public had picked up."

The durability of this true, dispassionately told tale emerges, perhaps, no more from the nightmare of injustice it reveals than from its stirring chronicle of the quiet, patient courage the defense committee displayed through the years and years of dedication which finally made that "dent on the public conscience."

And to what palpable dangers this little band of citizens exposed themselves by the temerity of their challenge to the System! The consistency of the State's hostility to their efforts was appalling, but characteristic of an anachronistic Establishment on the defensive: trial court judges with minds wizened by the past repeatedly denying defense efforts to include the full story of that July night in the record. A state's attorney, either by laxity or design, but at any rate made secure in the arrogance of his attitude by prevailing standards of justice in Maryland, suppressing evidence as to the character of the teen-aged "victim." Obscene "nigger-lover" calls to committee members in the dead of night. Harassment of them, subtle or overt, by local police and attachés of the sheriff's office; Such as the not quite Gestapo-like arrest of Harold Knapp, a government scientist and one of the most indefatigable of the defense volunteers, on a warrant charging disturbances of the peace and sworn out by the girl's mother—but not acted upon until eight days after it had been issued and, by coincidence, at 10 P.M. after a day of court hearings which had driven Knapp to bed in a state of near exhaustion.

No wonder that the brother of Alice Alt, another volunteer, anxiously asked her at one point, "Need you get so involved?" But these volunteers simply could not stay uninvolved, even though they were confronted with such hopeless circumstances as the bewildered reluctance of the parents of the Giles brothers to do anything. They were of the generation that "kept their place" and locked their mouths shut, no matter how deeply the wrongs against them rankled. As Frances Strauss reports with pointed poignancy, " . . . it never occurred to them that they had any personal rights."

Which brings to mind Edmund Burke's memorable observation that "for evil men to triumph it is necessary only for good men to do nothing." One is tempted to speculate that that piece of wisdom helped impel Winston Churchill to remind the British Parliament in the 1940's that democracy is the worst possible form of government—except all the others.

The lesson here is plain, yet one which it is not easy to forget, namely, that we cannot expect to enjoy the benefits of an open society without responding with the responsibility of personal participation.

Attorney Forer put it well in an extemporaneous résumé spoken to friends after their efforts had been finally crowned in quiet triumph with the full pardoning of the third defendant, Joe Johnson.

"I think that most of the people on the Giles-Johnson Defense Committee at the beginning," Forer said, "shared the kind of American view that our courts are infallible . . . somehow they think they can take some politician and put him on the bench and he'll get rid of all his prejudices, or turn into a genius, no matter how stupid he was before.

"Of course it's logical for people to feel that way; it makes them feel more comfortable to let the courts administer justice and handle life and death. . . . So it's easier to say 'Oh well, they'll settle it.' And that's one of the reasons why we don't have a better system for the administration of more justice."

It is a significant and potentially valuable coincidence that the chronicle of the Giles-Johnson case appears now, at a time when the American populace is riven with fear and hatred and weighted by the sloth of complacency. Through all the angry debate about separatism and integration, Lincoln's words again penetrate with the truth that this really *is* one nation, indivisible, and if we don't stand united we will fall divided.

"Where did the Justice go?"

"Someone asked Solon 2,500 years ago how justice could be achieved in Athens. His answer, in substance, was that justice could be achieved whenever those who were not injured by injustice were as outraged as those who had been."

—From a speech by Chief Justice Earl Warren at World Conference on World Peace Through the Rule of Law, July 1, 1963, Athens, Greece.

I

On summer evenings for as long as they could remember, the
three of them had met to swim and fish in the Patuxent. They
seldom bothered to go by the road. John and James Giles
would cut down through the fields from their house on the
ridge, and Joe Johnson from his. They liked best the place
where the river broadened out like a lake, and they had come
to feel that the stretch of water there, and the high, dense
woods bordering it were their territory, their backyard. If no
white people were swimming from the Rock, which thrust
out into the river from the bank at a height of twenty feet,
they took it over; if there were, or even if they found white
couples parked along the road, they would go upstream where
they could be alone.

That July night in 1961 started out like any other except
that John Bowie drove James Giles home from the place where
they had been laying sod, and the two of them went directly
to the river. Perhaps because it was Thursday, a week night,
they had the Rock all to themselves. Swimming led to fishing,
with a trip to the store to get a six-pack, some hooks and
sinkers, and a stop at Joe Johnson's for his lantern: it was
getting dark.

As they fished they didn't say much. John Giles never did
anyway. He was twenty-two, stocky like his younger brother,
with heavy, straight brows, a big nose, thick lips, and a neck

as round and strong as a column. He was moody, something of a solitary, shy and silent with people unless the talk turned to animals or snakes or plants or fish; then nobody could shut him up. When he worked, he worked hard, but he saw no sense in working day after day. All he wanted, and no more, was enough money to feed the animals he kept. He had stopped school after the seventh grade—too little "nature" talk.

His younger brother James had just graduated from high school. Almost twenty, he was a bit taller than John, and with a less rounded chin. He had the same neck, the same air of strength and solidity. But five extra years of education—the last in an integrated school—had left their mark. He was quicker, more alert and knowledgeable than John, more on to the ways of the world outside the tiny Negro community on the ridge.

Joe "Tiger" Johnson, third of the trio regularly at the river, was twenty-three. In his senior year in high school he had gone into the Army for fifteen months. Short and slender, with a narrow, pointed face, he was mercurial, and scrappy. He did not pick fights, but goaded or threatened beyond a certain point, he would let loose. He was particularly sensitive about his mother, who had gone into a mental hospital for good when he was nine. He had never forgotten the taunts that had come his way then, about her sanity and his. But none of this made much difference to the Giles brothers: they had known Joe all his life and viewed his scrappiness with tolerance.

By midnight they were ready to call it quits. They had to work the next day and besides, the river was now just barely discernible. The half-moon was close to the horizon, and beyond the glow of "Tiger's" lantern everything looked black. They picked up their catch—sunfish, blue gills, yellow perch, and some sizable catfish—and climbed up from the water's edge to the path that led back to the road. They felt as tranquil as the river they were leaving behind, and all except Bowie wanted to cut up through the woods to "Tiger" Johnson's yard where they always cleaned their fish, and then get to bed.

Bowie's car was where they had left it three hours before, almost nosed into the *No Trespassing* sign on the gate across the foot of Batson Road, if you could call that short narrow strip leading up to the highway a road. Bowie had aimed at backing up to the highway. But there on the left, sticking part-way into the lane, was a parked car. They could just make out the rear lights, one higher than the other as though the car had rolled down and had two wheels in the ditch. Lovers, probably. Who else ever parked there like that?

Well, one thing was sure. Bowie couldn't back up around that car without help. So the Giles* and Joe walked beside Bowie's car to guide him. As they drew alongside the parked car, they could make out two people in the back seat. A white boy called out the window, asking if they could get around. They could. Once in the clear, Bowie accelerated and got to the top, leaving the others behind. It was then that "Tiger," the unpredictable, lingered long enough by the parked car to ask for a cigarette. The boy said he didn't have one, and "Tiger" followed the Giles up the lane.

Bowie was waiting at the top on the main road. He still felt good from the beer and wanted to go dancing if anybody would go with him. No one would. They told him to go ahead; they could get back to "Tiger's" house quicker by the woods path, down by the gate. That settled it for Bowie. He was sleepy, too. He drove a little way along the highway, pulled off to the side, lay down on the seat, and within minutes was dead to the world and anything that might be happening on the road he had left behind.

* Everyone having anything to do with this case, including reporters, gave up at the start and called the Gileses the Giles, instead of using the correct plural.

"Where did the Justice go?"

As the three headed back down toward the shortcut, "Tiger" was in the lead. When he reached the parked car, he asked again for a cigarette, and with that repeated request, the whole incredible sequence of events began.

Later, not one of the three could remember in precisely the same way as the others the melee that followed. Yet they agreed on certain main points.*

Johnson got his cigarette. But as the white boy handed it out the window he yelled, "A cigarette isn't what you want, you black mother fucker, but whatever you want you're not going to get it. Now you get away from this car."

Joe pulled back. The Giles had now caught up with him.

"What's wrong? What's he saying?"

"He called me names."

More epithets came from the open window of the car.

"You don't have no cause to talk like that," John shouted in response.

"I've got three others coming back any minute," came from the car, "and they'll take care of you."

The three Negroes walked slightly away from the car.

"Are you going to take it?" James asked Joe.

"No," said Joe, and he went back to the window. "Call me that name again," he said, "and I'll drag your ass out of the car."

The boy called it again, wound up the car window, and ducked his head, but from within the car his muffled shouting could still be heard.

"The best thing you can do now is either get out of the car and fight or don't call me no more names."

* From here to the end of this chapter I have used a composite of the versions given by the Giles brothers and Joe Johnson on the witness stand. The white couple's versions were at variance. (Au.)

4

But the shouting went on. It was too much for Joe. In a raging determination "not to take it"—and joined now by James, who felt much the same—he grabbed whatever stones were loose on the lane and threw them with such force that they smashed the windows on the road side of the car. As they did so, the door on the woods side opened and someone ran off into the woods. On their side, the white boy got out, ready for a fight, but one blow of fist or rock from "Tiger" Johnson knocked him to the ground.

He lay very still, blood spurting from around his mouth. Joe and James Giles stood looking down at him. Then, with one impulse, they turned away, wanting only to collect John and get away from that spot.

John was not in sight. They called him and walked into the woods, but they could not see him and came back to the road where the white boy still lay beside the car. James bent over him, holding in his hand a stick that he had picked up in the woods, to see how badly the boy was hurt. He was surprised to discover that the boy was about his own age. He was conscious now.

"Don't hurt me," said the boy.

"I'm not going to hurt you," said James.

"Here's a quarter. It's all I have."

James pocketed the quarter and set off into the woods to try again to find John and go home.

In the black woods, the underbrush crackling as they walked, they heard a girl call, "Where have you been so long?" and they followed the sound to where they found John and the girl sitting together. It was too dark to see more than that she was white. She seemed very friendly and kept laughing, as though she were not at all alarmed by the situation.

"I know what you boys want," she said. "I've already had sixteen or seventeen this week and three more won't make any difference. Since you were the one to find me," she said to John, "you can be first." Then she took off her shorts and underpants, carefully folded them, and laid them on the ground beside her.

They were mystified. How were they supposed to act when a girl behaved like that? Had John made some arrangement with her before they had arrived? But John was the most puzzled. He had never known such a girl, and more than that, he had shied away from white women all his life. In the ten minutes or so they had been alone, she had kept on chatting as though she had always known him, telling him she was on probation, and since John himself was in trouble—for a minor offense to be sure, but it had put him on probation also—he had felt sorry for her.

Was John first? He said afterwards that he had never touched her; James confirmed it, and added that the girl herself had said so that night. But at first Johnson said John had tried and failed. In any event, John shortly disappeared into the woods.

So Joe Johnson, then, took his turn, finished, and went home to bed. Then James began, ignoring his brother, who had returned and was saying, "Come on, let's go"; seeing it was useless, John went away again. Both James and the girl ignored, as well, the shouted words of her escort, back on the lane, that he was going for the police.

James was still lying with her when he heard police sirens, and suddenly saw lights flashing through the treetops over their heads. He got up, pulled on his clothes, and fled toward the river. As he ran, he remembered she had said she was in trouble, and if she were found there, she would have to claim rape.

A few minutes later—about 1:00 in the morning—she was found.

6

When William Rogers got to his feet from where he had been lying on Batson Road, he ran to the Cunningham's, the only house anywhere near. He saw no lights, but his frantic knocking soon brought Mr. Cunningham to the door. "Give me a gun," said William. "Three niggers have got my girl." Instead, Mr. Cunningham called the police. William started back to the road when they heard the sound of the sirens. Then Mr. Cunningham dressed and walked down to the scene, arriving just as William and the police sergeant brought the girl out from the woods, below the trees that looked yellow-green in the revolving lights of the police car. Shortly afterward an ambulance came to take the girl and William to the hospital, she for an examination, and he to have stitches around his mouth. On Batson Road the police radioed for dogs and began their careful photographing of the car and its contents, their flashguns popping off in steady succession. The search had begun.

Actually, there proved little need for either the dogs or a lengthy search. For there was Bowie, in his car not far away on the highway above, far gone in the sleep of a twenty-five-year-old who had topped a day of hard physical work with six hours of swimming and fishing. He had heard nothing, seen nothing, known nothing, and when the police shone their lights in his face he woke—bewildered and almost blinded—to try to grasp what they wanted. At first he proved a "reluctant" witness, but when they took him to the station he began to talk—fumbling and guarded talk. He said one of his fishing companions "resembled" the Giles brothers, and a guard was dispatched to the Giles's house under surveillance. He said the other—well, all he knew was that they called him "Tiger." Was that their beer, up at the Rock? Where had they got it? And from the owner of the Red Door Store, the police easily learned the identity of "Tiger."

. . . And here come two detectives, coming in [testified Joe Johnson]. One of them woke me up and asked me, "Is your name Johnson?" I said, "Yes." . . . They said, "Well come along with me. Put your clothes on. I want to ask you some questions." . . . Before I got in the car the first thing he said was, "We never take nobody in without handcuffs so we just as well put them on him too." So I go down, no, before I get to the station they stopped at James Giles house because this car radioed to watch for them because they had trailed them up that far almost to his house. So we pulled in James's lane and turned the car around and headed out of the lane and just about that time here comes Jim walking across the yard . . .

(He had been walking all night in the woods. Now, at shortly before seven in the morning, he reached home exhausted, his clothes drenched and his shoes soaked.)

. . . and there is a police standing by the door of the house and Detective Harding jumps out of the car . . . and this other police takes Jim into the house and makes him change his clothes also. So he changed his clothes and he come back out and he got almost to Detective Harding from the house, which was about fifteen to twenty more feet between Kennedy, . . . the Detective that had me and the first thing he said was, "Don't look at him. Don't say nothing to him." . . . So I slides over . . . on the left hand side of the driver's side of the car in the back seat and Jim sit directly behind the passenger seat. So we go down to the station and he put both of us in this cell. They put Jim in this end of the cell block and put me up this end because they said it would be best for you all not to say nothing to each other, like that.

John was not seen until Sunday afternoon, some sixty-two hours after he had left his brother and the girl. He had kept moving steadily through the denseness of the woods along the river, only once having anything to eat when he cooked a frog he had caught over a fire. Finally he had decided to give himself up and went to stand in front of a gas station in a

nearby town. The detectives questioned him from 3:00 till
7:45 P.M. ("Admits first to find the girl but did not have anything to do with her . . . we were unable to shake his story,"
read the report.)

Though each went through the experience at a different
time, the procedure was much the same. First came the line-up
for identification, taking place for James and Joe "Tiger" Johnson within an hour or so after they had been brought to the
police station. With other Negroes of roughly the same height
and build, each stood in line for the confrontation with Stella
Mae Watkins. She was brought to the doorway and stood
there to look them over. They stared back in astonishment:
could *that* be the girl who had chatted so confidently and
knowingly with them in the woods? Why, she did not seem
like a girl at all, but like a thin and wan child whose long,
dyed-blond hair framed a face drained of any color.

The line-up rankled all three, each insisting that Stella Mae
had been helped in the identification. "She was told my name
and where I lived," said James. "They called my name right
off," said John, "and I think the girl should know my name
by then."

But only Joe Johnson, faced with that unexpectedly strange
person, claimed that he—in turn—could not have identified
her. State's Attorney Kardy questioned him:

> Q. And when they asked you in Stella Watkins' presence
> there at the lineup whether you had ever seen her before
> you said no?
> A. That's right.
> Q. That wasn't true was it?
> A. Sure it was true.
> Q. You had never seen her before?
> A. No, not to know her by just looking at her again that
> day.
> Q. You mean to tell this Court and these Gentlemen of the
> Jury you are on top of a woman, longwinded, on there

9

for about ten minutes or so, having intercourse with her, I suppose you are in a normal position, she being on the bottom and you being on the top, is that the position you were in?

A. Yes.

Q. Was your face next to hers?

A. Probably so.

Q. And you didn't know who it was?

A. Not to recognize. Not to be able to walk in a room and point you or you or you out, and say that's the one.

Nevertheless, Stella had made the correct identifications. Fingerprinting was done; warrants were read; statements always "freely and voluntarily given" were duly taken down. The police never "made any threats, promises or inducements" to the defendants. The procedure went along at a fast clip, almost automatically. "Directing your attention to the day of . . ." "Did you have any further conversation with . . ." "Were his statements . . ." "Who was present . . ." "Did there come a time when . . ." And so on, through every shred of fact and each point of time, through every separate routine in which the police officers had been schooled.

True, two detectives remembered matters with a slight difference. One said Joe Johnson had been advised of his right to a lawyer—"Object," said the State's Attorney. "That's not a rule in Maryland. Object."—and the other said he had *not* been advised either of his right to remain silent or to have a lawyer. But in general the police knew the Maryland legal ropes, and proceeded with their interrogation. Then they wrote a statement, which the defendants did not hear, read, or sign.

II

IN THE CIRCUIT COURT FOR MONTGOMERY COUNTY,
MARYLAND

STATE OF MARYLAND   )
            Plaintiff,   :

      Vs.   )   No. 4590 Criminals.

JAMES V. GILES and   :
JOHN G. GILES,   )

         Defendants.

                   :
— — — — — — — X

The above-entitled action came on regularly for trial, pursuant to notice, on December 4, 1961, at 9:30 A.M. before The Honorable James H. Pugh, Judge of said Court, and a jury, when and where the following counsel were present on behalf of the respected parties and the following proceedings were had and the following testimony was adduced.

APPEARANCES

> Leonard T. Kardy, State's Attorney
> James Cromwell, Assistant State's Attorney,
>   on behalf of the plaintiff,
> Stedman Prescott, Jr.,
>   on behalf of the defendants.

The trial of No. 4590 Criminals was held in Rockville, Maryland, in the "new" courthouse, a mass of heavy gray stone adjoining the red-brick building which had served Montgomery County for well over half a century.

Courtroom #1 was large and awesomely formal, with dark, burnished walnut paneling and velvet maroon drapes. The high black leather chair reserved for the judge was flanked by the American and Maryland flags. To the right of the bench— from the spectators' point of view—were the witness box and the tiers of seats reserved for the jury; below it, in front, sat the court reporter and a clerk, and on the floor were the tables for the lawyers.

On that December morning in 1961, the large room was nearly empty except for those directly concerned and the regular members of the jury panel who sat awaiting the challenging which would probably send most of them back to their jobs or homes. No one from the press was there, or expected.

The Giles filled much of the fifth row (Joe Johnson was to be tried separately, later). Mr. Giles was burly and heavy-set, almost sixty, some twelve years older than his wife, who was plump and comfortable looking, with a pretty light-brown face and reddish hair. But she was not well—diabetes and a heart condition—and the strain was evident. Of their seven children, only three were beside her today, the others being away or at work. At the far end sat Caleb Adams, Mrs. Giles's uncle and patriarch of the family which had lived in the Spencerville area, not far from the Patuxent River, for three generations— maybe more. "They weren't great for keeping records in those days," said Caleb Adams.

In the section on the other side of the aisle, in the front row, sat Mrs. Watkins, a short, forty-five-year-old woman with very black hair, dark, opaque eyes, and tightly compressed lips. Her son John, a policeman—as was Stella's other brother— sat beside her because her much older husband—soon to retire —was at work that day.

By 9:20, the lawyers had exchanged greetings and begun
sorting into piles the papers they took from their briefcases.
At 9:25, the sheriff, a tall and surprisingly benign-looking
man, brought in the Giles brothers—dark trousers, jackets
over their white shirts, John with his head bent slightly, James
with his head held high, both straight-browed like their great-
uncle Caleb. Handcuffed together, they walked awkwardly,
their eyes searching the courtroom for their family. They had
just time to give them fleeting smiles before they were seated
at the front, their handcuffs removed and their backs to the
courtroom. Their court-appointed lawyer, Stedman Prescott,
went to shake their hands and then returned to his table.

Precisely when the big clock on the front wall showed 9:30,
the clerk banged his gavel—"All rise, please"—and Judge
Pugh entered and walked quickly to his high leather chair.
In his late fifties, almost entirely bald, lean, and tight-faced,
he was impatient of delay and sharp with anyone occasioning
it. "He's pleasant enough when you meet him socially," was
the going verdict, "and good on zoning cases, but he's hell on
crime."

Stedman Prescott first noted for the record that there were
no Negroes on the regular panel of jurors, and then began
challenging. Though each juror answered "No" to the question: "Do any one of you have any bias or prejudice with
respect to the Negro race, such as would preclude you from
giving a Negro a fair and impartial trial, as you would a white
man?" Prescott challenged thirty-one to the State's three, and
the regular panel was then exhausted. The sheriff was dispatched to "summon six talesmen" from people standing in
the corridor or on the street outside; and after more challenging, the jury was at last seated, the witnesses were ordered to
leave the room, and most of the rejected jurors left as well.
The State's Attorney for Montgomery County then rose and

walked confidently toward the juror's box to make his opening statement.

Leonard Kardy was about forty, running a bit to fat now, so that his bright blue suit stretched tight at the seams. He had tightly curling black hair, a round, boyish face, large brown eyes, and a deep dimple in his chin. Originally from New Jersey, he had been Deputy State's Attorney for Montgomery County and then had become State's Attorney in 1958, the same year in which Judge Pugh was elected to the bench, and was up for office the second time, with the election a month hence. His handling of a jury was adroit: he would lull them into an almost hypnotic trance with his short, vivid, emotion-laden words, and then—by introducing deliberately chosen vulgarities or startling images—would jerk them back into a surprised attention.

Today he quickly covered the preliminaries, introducing himself, his assistant Cromwell, and the defense lawyer Prescott. The case, he said, involved an indictment containing three counts: rape; assault with intent to rape; and assault and battery. (He did not mention a count having to do with "robbery," occasioned by James's pocketing the quarter handed to him by William.) He told the ages of the defendants and of the juvenile Stella Mae—sixteen—and located the scene: "Batson Road runs back into a woods, a lonely, desolate area; a very heavily wooded area in that part of the County." He said that "Stella Mae Watkins and her friend, William Rogers, went down to that area in a motor vehicle . . . and when they got down there, they ran out of gas and Stella Mae Watkins and her friend, William Rogers, remained in the back seat of this motor vehicle." He continued with an account of what happened on the road that night and how the three Negroes had asked William for

> . . . some money, and he said he had no money except cigarette money and they said "Well, if that is the case, we are

going to take your girl from you" and they got rocks and
started breaking locks. The car was locked and in the car was
the Watkins girl and the Rogers boy and the testimony will
show that these two, along with the Johnson boy, started
breaking the windows of the car . . . and they shouted to this
boy that they were going to shoot him and they wanted this
girl in the car. As they were breaking in the window the
Rogers boy told the girl to make a run for it and he would
try to hold these three off. They broke in the rear window . . .
and the Rogers boy jumped out and was hit in the side of the
mouth with a brick or a stone, rendering him at least par-
tially unconscious. He fell to the ground bleeding and when
he awoke in a few minutes, he found James Giles standing
over him with a stick and asking for his money and he gave
him a quarter. In the meantime the girl, Stella Mae Watkins,
made a run for it, and started going through this deep woods,
this lonely desolate area off Spencerville, and she fell to the
ground, having tripped over something, and she lay there
silent and still, and the testimony will show that then John
Giles came through the woods, looking for her, and running
after her.

He paused for a moment, his face solemn, and then went on:

He found her there in the woods and he got down on top of
her and told her to be quiet and he said "I am going to call
the other boys" . . . and he said "Will you give me some if I
don't call them?" and she said "Yes, if we go down deeper in
the woods" and the testimony will show that the other two boys
back up at that car, standing over that bleeding boy, started
coming into the woods . . . and looking for the girl. The testimony will show that there was a noise in the woods and
these two boys, James Giles and the Johnson boy, heard this
noise and found John Giles on top of the girl there in the
woods and there was an argument that ensued . . . as to who
was going to have intercourse with her first. It was decided
that John would have it first, because he found her . . . John
Giles did have intercourse with her and after he finished with
the girl, she down there with her pants off her, her shorts off
her and her moccasins off, and nothing on but a blouse,

15

> Joseph Johnson got on her and he had intercourse with her
> and thereafter James Giles got on top of her and he proceeded
> to have intercourse with her, and while he was on top of her
> and having intercourse with her there were headlights that
> came into the area and when those headlights came into the
> area, we will show you that this was a police car and these
> boys ran from the scene.

He went on through the remainder of that night and what
happened subsequently at the police station:

> They were brought to the Wheaton-Glenmont station and
> interrogated. James Giles said he was at the scene and that
> was all he would say until he was confronted by Joseph John-
> son . . . he readily admitted then that he was at the scene; he
> said they all agreed, that being Johnson, John Giles and him-
> self, James Giles, agreed they were going to get some pussy.
> He said that was agreed when they were talking behind the
> car. They knew there was a boy in there and that there was
> a girl in there, too, and they agreed they were going to get
> some pussy.

Next he talked of the line-ups for identification of James
and Joe; then he brought John into the picture, saying first
how Stella Mae had picked him out of two line-ups.

> John Giles was interrogated by the police. He said he was
> there, but didn't know anything about getting any pussy but
> told them "I did break into the car." . . . After that interro-
> gation by the Montgomery County police his brother was
> brought into his presence and he said "You know we all
> agreed to get some pussy" and this boy just shook his head.
>   Now upon showing you all these facts, ladies and gentle-
> men, and we will offer the evidence right down the line and
> let you hear this case in its true light . . . we will ask you
> to bring back the only verdict possible in this case, guilty
> under the first count, of rape.

Kardy sat down and Prescott got slowly to his feet.
Maryland-bred, the son of a judge, he was a different type of

person from Kardy altogether: conservatively dressed, with a fleshy but not at all boyish face, and intelligent blue eyes.

All the cards were stacked against him—including the fact that he had not been appointed until well on into November—and he knew it. He had gone at once to the jail and there interviewed the Giles and Joe Johnson separately.

He emerged sufficiently impressed with the similarity of their stories to feel that they might be innocent of rape—in the technical sense. Proof was a different matter, and Mrs. Giles and Mr. Cunningham—to whose house William had run that night—were the only two people he succeeded in interviewing, and he thought that their words would have little effect on a jury. At Stella Mae's house, her mother told him she would have to consult Lieutenant Whelan, a detective of the Montgomery County police, before she could give him permission to interview her daughter. When he called back, she said Whelan's answer was "No." He was unable to locate William Rogers. No transcript of the preliminary hearing existed, because transcripts cost money and the Giles had spared all they could afford to hire a lawyer to defend their sons at that hearing. That lawyer had told Prescott all he could remember, but it remained, legally speaking, hearsay.

Then, remembering how the three had quoted Stella Mae as saying she was "in trouble" and "on probation," he went to the juvenile courts of both Montgomery County, where the episode had taken place, and Prince George's County, where Stella lived. Did they have any records on her? "We do not release the records of juveniles," he was told.

So he had nothing to go on but the boys' stories, and the contents of Kardy's file on the case, which Kardy had shown him. He began his opening statement knowing that it would be an anticlimax—as indeed it was. "In this case we expect to show you that this thing happened very much as Mr. Kardy has told you," and Prescott, too, sketched the events of the night; but he said that William Rogers had shouted racial epithets at the three, and that when James and Joe found John and Stella sitting together, she had said, "I know what you want," had removed and folded her own clothes, and had directed the order in which they might have intercourse with her.

> She turned to these boys and said "Fellows, look; I am on probation . . . for this type of act" and she said "If the police come, I am going to have to say I was raped . . ." We expect to show you that no one held that girl there; that there was no fight; no struggle at the scene. She didn't scream; she didn't holler. She didn't protest in any way. She didn't even ask them not to do it . . . She didn't do anything to protect her so-called Honor, we expect your finding to be Not Guilty.

The State's first witness was John Bowie, who had gone to sleep in his car parked on the highway above Batson Road. He was uncomfortable and miserable on the witness stand, unhappy about his part in the whole affair, and did not let his eyes wander to where the Giles brothers were sitting. His testimony added nothing new.

William Rogers came next—short, slender, red-haired, with an air of pleasing deference and "clean-cut" openness. His eyes moved continuously, but since he faced the lawyers rather than the jury, the habit passed unnoticed. Cromwell, Kardy's assistant, questioned him, following the preliminaries of name, address, and occupation, with asking him what he had done "on the evening of July 20, 1961?"

> A. Well I had a date with Stella and I went down and picked her up . . . around 10:30 when I picked her up.
> Q. Day or night?
> A. That night and we talked to a few of her friends and we were supposed to meet them up at the Rock on Batson Road . . . and we went on up there and when we got

there we found some people up there that was hung up
in a ditch.

Q. Who was with you?

A. Mark White, Sammy Harper, Stella and myself.

Q. Approximately at what time did you arrive on Batson
Road?

A. I guess about 11:30.

Stella and he were riding in the back seat, and when they
reached the road they found another car, "hung up in a ditch."
(State's Exhibit #3 was handed to Rogers to identify where
the other car had been "hung up.") They helped the car, and
then, discovering their own car was out of gas, they arranged
that White would go with the other car, along with Sammy
Harper, to get some gas. They pushed White's car "on off
Batson Road, on to a little dirt road that runs down to the
river," and in it William and Stella stayed while the others
went for gas. Then Bowie's car was guided past them, "and
I locked the doors and I got a little bit shaken up."

Q. Why?

A. Well, I don't know; three subjects getting out of a car
and coming down towards us, and I didn't know what
was going to happen, just Stella and I there by ourselves
. . . and I could hear this mumbling and they came
back up and said they wanted the girl.

Q. What did you say?

A. And I said "You aren't going to get the girl" and they
said "Well I will kill your fucking ass" and I heard a
brick go through the window and one of them said
"Let's shoot the son-of-a-bitch."

And so on it went, including State's Exhibits for Rogers to
identify and other legal necessities. Then Mr. Prescott rose to
cross-examine:

Q. How long had you known Stella Mae Watkins?

A. I don't know. It was a right good while.

Q. How often did you date her?

A. I was dating her regular.

Q. Did you all make a habit of going on dates, starting at 10:30 in the evening?

. . . . .

A. No. I was just a little late getting down there. Mark first went to pick up his girl, and I was late getting to Stella's house.

Q. Was Mark's girl friend with you on this occasion?

A. No. She couldn't come.

Q. So you and some other guy named Sammy Harper, and Stella, all went out to this spot in the woods; is that right?

A. We were supposed to meet some of her girl friends.

Q. Who were they?

A. I don't know their names.

Q. How do you know you were supposed to meet them?

A. We were talking to them after I picked up Stella.

. . . . .

Q. Did you all have your bathing suits with you that evening?

A. I had mine in the car, and Mark had his in the car.

Q. Did Stella have hers with her?

A. I guess she did, but I don't know.

. . . . .

Q. And Mark just left his car out there with you and Stella?

A. He was coming back after he got the gas.

Q. Did he ever come back?

A. I don't know because I wasn't there. They took us away in the ambulance.

. . . . .

Q. What did you three boys take Stella out there for that night?

A. I told you we were going to meet some friends up there and go swimming.

Q. You didn't take her out there to have sexual relations with her, yourself, did you?

"Where did the Justice go?"

* Mr. Cromwell: Objection.
The Court: Overruled.
A.   No.

. . . . .

Q.   This was a heavily wooded area, wasn't it?
A.   Yes, sir; to the right of us it was.
Q.   Really on both sides, it is heavily wooded, isn't it?
A.   Well it is kind of thick on that side because it grows up
in honeysuckle.
Q.   You wouldn't say there is woods on both sides?
A.   Further down, yes, but there is mostly honeysuckle right
there.
Q.   At any time did you ever hear Stella scream, or holler
out?
A.   I think I heard her voice a couple of times.
Q.   You didn't hear her calling for help, or screaming, did
you?
A.   I just heard that whimpering noise.
Q.   You told her you were going for the police?
A.   Yes, I called out to her that I was going to get some help.
Q.   She didn't tell you to hurry up, did she?
A.   No. She didn't say anything.
Q.   Did you recall telling these boys that there were three
other boys with you, rather than two?
A.   No. I didn't tell them anything.
Q.   You remember cussing them out, don't you?
A.   I did not do that.
Q.   You didn't call them "black mother fuckers"?
A.   No, I did not.
Q.   Are you sure you didn't say that?
A.   No. I know better than to say something like that when
there were three of them against me.

. . . . .

Q.   None of you went down toward the river, did you?
A.   No, sir.
Q.   And yet you went out there to go swimming?
A.   That is right.

* In the legal transcripts of the Giles's trial the word "By" appears
before the names of speakers. (Au.)

Mr. Prescott: I have no further questions.

The Court: Is that all?

Mr. Cromwell: That is all, your Honor.

The Court: You may step down.

The Court: During the recess, ladies and gentlemen, you will not discuss this case among yourselves, or allow anybody to discuss it in your presence. We will recess for luncheon until 1:30 P.M. Is there any request to have the jury locked up, gentlemen?

Mr. Prescott: No, your Honor.

(Luncheon recess)

III

By 1:30 that afternoon the trial was again in full swing. The doctor who had examined Stella Mae in the early, pre-dawn hours of July 21 gave his testimony in three minutes; the testimony of the doctor who had stitched Roger's mouth was equally brief. The State next called Mr. Cunningham, to whose house William had run for help, and soon finished with him.

Prescott rose to cross-examine. Cunningham was his only source of admittedly impartial evidence and, furthermore, he had the poised presence of a successful man. What he might say could conceivably implant some doubt in the minds of the jurors, who were mostly "up-country" types. But Cromwell, Kardy's assistant, broke in repeatedly.

> Q.   How did the girl appear to you, sir; did she appear to be shaken up at all?
> Mr. Cromwell: I object.
> The Court: Overruled.
> A.   Do you mean physically?
> Q.   Physically or mentally; either one.
> Mr. Cromwell: He certainly cannot testify to the mental state. I object.
> The Court: Just describe the physical appearance as you saw it.
> A.   She walked out of the woods, with the Sergeant assisting her, and walked across to the car, where he told her to

> sit down in the car. She was not hysterical, if that is
> what you mean.
> Q.   Did she appear to be disturbed in any way?
> A.   I don't know if I can honestly answer that. To me there
> was not an immediate obvious sign of disturbance, but I
> am not qualified to judge that.
> Q.   Did she appear to be cool, calm and collected?
> Mr. Cromwell: Objection.
> The Court: Overruled.
> A.   I would say yes.

But Cromwell saw to it that these words did not remain
uncontested in the minds of the jurors, and Mr. Cunningham,
an intellectually honest man, helped him to obliterate them.

> Q.   Mr. Cunningham, could you tell from your observation
> . . . what her emotional state was . . . ?
> A.   I don't think I can say that about anyone.

The door to the witness box opened next to admit Stella
Mae. Prescott's face showed his dismay at her appearance.
She looked like a child of 12, just a wisp of a girl; thin, flat-
chested, white-faced, and with lank blond hair hanging to her
shoulders. A skeptical jury might reason that any girl as
patently lacking in sexual appeal as this one could only achieve
dates because of her availability. A skeptical jury might wonder, as well, why "this little girl" was found after midnight
on Batson Road with a boy five years older in that "lonely and
desolate area," and might also question the contradiction between that child-like exterior and the self-possession with
which she gave her answers.

But this was not a skeptical jury. Furthermore, jurors were
likely to assume that any hesitation to answer on the part of a
witness meant that he needed time to formulate a lie; prompt
replies, on the other hand, they found convincing.

Stella spoke softly, telling how the "three colored males" had
said they wanted William's girl and he had said, "You are going

to have to kill me first"; how he had used no profanity whatsoever; how she had run into the woods "about thirty feet,"
tripped, was out of breath, and could not run anymore, "so I
tried to lay there and be as quiet as I could." She recalled no
conversation with John Giles and she had herself unzipped the
shorts she was wearing when the three threatened to do so.

A.   I was completely dazed. There wasn't anyone to yell to
     for help; there wasn't anything I could do, and they
     were all three standing around me.
Q.   Did you scream?
A.   No, there wasn't any sense in screaming.

John had been first, she said, and quickly went on to answer
the rest of Kardy's questions.

Rising to cross-examine, Prescott hoped to break down her
self-possession, and asked if her parents let her go out at any
time of night she wanted, a question which was promptly objected to, and the objection sustained. And what had happened
to the others who were supposed to be joining them? Where
was her bathing suit? ("My girl friend had it in her car.")
And she insisted she had never discussed the case with William
Rogers, though she had had dates with him after the night on
Batson Road.

Q.   Now you recall testifying at the preliminary hearing in
     this case?
A.   Yes, sir.
Q.   Do you recall telling the Court there that only two of
     these boys had intercourse with you?
A.   I recall saying that intercourse was had three times.
Q.   Did you tell them only with two of the boys?
A.   I was confused.

There followed the objections, that Prescott had anticipated,
on the grounds that anything he had been told by the lawyer at
the preliminary hearing was "hearsay." The judge told him to
rephrase his questions.

Q. Why are you telling a different story today than the story you told the police immediately after this happened, and the story you told at the preliminary hearing?
A. Because I have thought about it.
Q. What do you mean you have thought about it?
A. Well at the time I was confused—people were giving names, and I had no idea of what the boys' names were.
Q. Who was given names?
A. After the line-ups; after I had identified all three . . .
Q. As a matter of fact, at the line-up you were able to identify them because they called them by names . . . isn't that so?
A. No, sir.

· · · · ·

Q. And you were confused at that time, and you later learned that they all had names and then you decided that all three of them had intercourse with you; is that correct?
A. No.
Q. What did you think?
A. I don't recall now what I thought.
Q. And you want to tell a different story here from what you told at the preliminary hearing?

· · · · ·

A. I only told the truth.
Q. And you weren't telling the truth before; is that right?
A. Yes.

Prescott then switched the subject and, over objections, finally established the fact that she had been in the same spot with Rogers before. The three had not mistreated her, she admitted, but repeated that they were all "standing around." Again Prescott shifted the ground of his questioning:

Q. Stella, have you ever been convicted of a crime, yourself?
Mr. Kardy: Object.
The Court: Do you proffer to prove anything other than a juvenile offense?

Mr. Prescott: No, your Honor.

The Court: It wouldn't be admissible.

Mr. Prescott: I believe I am entitled to show if she has a record.

The Court: Approach the Bench, gentlemen.

(*Bench Conference*)

The Court: Read the question back.

The Reporter: "Stella, have you ever been convicted of a crime, yourself?"

A.   Yes, sir.

Q.   What was that crime?

A.   Running away from home.

Mr. Kardy: Oh, your Honor, that is no crime.

The Court: Is that all you have been convicted of?

A.   Yes, sir.

The Court: . . . That is a juvenile matter. So your answer would be that other than that, no . . .

.   .   .   .   .

Q.   Stella, do you recall telling these boys that you had intercourse with sixteen other boys that week . . .

.   .   .   .   .

A.   I did not tell them that.

Q.   Do you recall telling these boys that you were on probation and if you were caught by the police you would have to tell them that you were raped?

A.   No, sir.

Q.   You didn't say that, either?

A.   No, sir.

Q.   Stella, how do you think these boys knew you were on probation, if you didn't tell them that?

To this there was no answer, because Judge Pugh sustained the State's objection. After a few more questions, Prescott finished and Kardy rose to ask Stella whether she had been on probation that night; she had not, she said, and she had only let the boys have intercourse with her because "they had chased me and I was afraid for my life."

John was put on the stand first, told his story, and then was cross-examined by Kardy:

Q. Why would you go into the woods when the girl went into the woods?
A. I went over into the path.
Q. Is that where you found the girl?
A. I didn't find her; she found me . . . . She asked me to help her.

. . . . .

Q. Now, here we are, about 1:30 in the morning, over there on Batson Road and your brother, James, and Johnson pushing in the windows, and it is your testimony that you just walked down the path and you met a girl you had never seen before . . . and the first words out of her mouth were "I am on a year's probation and I don't want to get in any trouble and I have had sexual intercourse with sixteen or seventeen boys this week anyway and two or three won't make any difference."
A. That is right.
Q. Did she insist that you have intercourse with her?
A. She did . . . . She said "If you will help me, you can be first" and she started laughing . . . she asked me to lead her away from that spot.
Q. Did you lead her away?
A. We started and made some noise and then we sat down.

. . . . .

Q. So you were on probation and she was on probation and so you just sat down and talked?
A. Yes . . . . She was doing all the talking.

John's testimony concluded the first day, and when James testified the next morning he did not deviate from John's story. He was followed by the only remaining witness, their father, who testified that he had never had any trouble with the two boys and that they had always "worked good."

Leonard Kardy said the State would withdraw all counts other than the first, that of rape, and the judge then briefly instructed the jury—which in Maryland is the judge of law as well as of fact—in the following words:

> Now, ladies and gentlemen of the jury, the form of your verdict in this case will simply be "Guilty on the First Count" or "Guilty on the First Count without capital punishment" or "Not Guilty," as you shall find from the law and the evidence. You will make a finding as to each defendant under that instruction. Since the lunch hour has arrived we have ordered your lunch and it will be available when you retire to your jury room. Swear the Bailiff.

So the jury ate and considered and returned in an hour with the verdict "Guilty on the First Count." Judge Pugh stated he would sentence five days hence, on Monday, and the session was adjourned. The Giles family went back to their home in Spencerville and their sons back to Seven Locks jail, on the road outside Rockville.

On Monday, Prescott produced one witness who said the brothers were "good workers. You could leave them by themselves and they kept right on working. . . . They seemed to be honest and straightforward." No one else spoke, because Judge Pugh had ordered no pre-sentencing investigation.

> Mr. Prescott: That is all I have to offer. If it please your Honor, of course I realize the seriousness and the nature of this charge . . . but I certainly feel that this is a case in which the death sentence should not apply and I sincerely request your Honor not to impose the death sentence . . . in this case. They are both young men and they had a good record up until now, and I feel that if your Honor were lenient with them they can in the future make good citizens of the State and the community.
>
> Judge Pugh: James V. Giles, stand up. Have you reason to assign why the Court should not proceed to sentence you in No. 4590 Criminals, in which you have been found

guilty by the jury of the crime of rape? Anything you want to say?

James Giles: No, sir.

Judge Pugh: I might say to you, Giles, that the verdict of the jury in this case was fully justified under the evidence. You have been convicted of a most serious offense. The crime of rape of a woman has been placed in the same category as murder in the first degree, when the facts justify an unqualified verdict, such as has been rendered by the Jury in this case.

The law protects a woman from unwarranted attacks against her person. You have also violated the natural law of decency, as well as the statute law of this State. Your passionate desire to carnally know this sixteen-year-old girl led you to commit violence against her escort, his person and property. You were so ravenous that nothing could prevent your committing this treacherous act. You were determined to satisfy your passionate desires.

The Jury has placed the responsibility for your future in my hands. I shall not evade it. The purpose of a sentence is twofold: first, to mete out the punishment for the crime committed, and second, to deter others from committing a like offense. By your vicious act, you are not entitled to any consideration by this Court.

It is the sentence of this Court that you, James V. Giles, be taken into custody by the Sheriff of this County and held by him in solitary confinement; that under such guard or guards as he shall determine to be necessary, and as soon hereafter as possible, the said Sheriff shall deliver you to the Warden of the Maryland Penitentiary, where you shall be placed in solitary confinement under such guard or guards as shall be necessary, until such time as the warrant directing your execution shall name, when you shall suffer death by the administration of a lethal gas —and may God have mercy on your soul.

·   ·   ·   ·   ·

John G. Giles, stand up. Do you have any reason to assign why the Court should not proceed to sentence you in

No. 4590 Criminals, in which you have been found guilty
by the jury of the crime of rape? Anything you want to say?

John G. Giles: I do.

Judge Pugh: What do you have to say?

John G. Giles: Well, the girl said I didn't rape her. I said
I didn't rape her and they said I didn't rape her, and so
that is all.

.   .   .   .   .

Judge Pugh: Of course the jury didn't believe you; and the
jury rightly didn't believe you. What I have said to your
brother . . . applies to you . . . lethal gas—and may God
have mercy on your soul.

The next day the Giles brothers were removed from Seven
Locks jail. Each was fitted into a broad leather belt, his wrists
handcuffed to the steel ring hanging from its locked clasp, and
led to the waiting black police wagon. Inside, guards sat beside
them, and through the small, high window in the rear of the
van, they could see nothing of the countryside, nor of the city
of Baltimore as they approached it, nor of the front of the
imposing, fortress-like granite building which had served Maryland as its "maximum security" penitentiary for more than a
century. They were driven through a gate in the high, thick
wall surrounding the area, and led to their separate cells in the
tier known as Death Row.

IV

Frances Ross was seven when her family moved to Peking, where her father became an adviser to the Chinese government and where—"my family was always very church-oriented"— they lived in the Mission Compound. In 1927 she entered Carleton College in Minnesota, working for three years after graduation for the League of Women Voters and going on to take a master's degree in Public Administration. Howard Ross took his degree in the same subject, and after their marriage and some years in the Midwest, the war brought them to Washington and a government job for Howard.

They lived first in Prince George's County, and then in Montgomery, and while their daughters were young, Frances Ross's life revolved around the P.T.A., Campfire Girls, and 4-H clubs. But once the girls had gone off to preparatory school, she returned to work again with the League of Women Voters —this time as a volunteer—in her church, and in politics.

"I don't like politics," she said, "but I've come to realize you can't do anything without it."

On the Tuesday morning of December 21, 1961, the Rosses were eating breakfast in the kitchen, as they usually did, he sitting on the long, padded bench built into the wall and she —when the eggs were done and the coffee ready—on a chair across from him. Out of habit he flipped through the first section of the *Washington Post* and then propped it against the

toaster to read any international news related to his civil
service job in Washington. Out of habit she extracted the section on Area News, where there was certain to be information
on Montgomery County. They spoke little. During twenty-five
years of marriage they had learned to postpone most conversation till dinnertime.

At 7:40, as he started to leave, briefcase in hand, he said,
"You don't suppose those are our Giles, do you? You'll find it
on page three. Two Giles brothers got the death sentence yesterday for rape."

"Oh, I don't think they could be Mary's sons. I asked her
one day this fall what her boys were doing and she said, 'Anything they can find to do.' "

"Probably some other Giles. There are lots of Giles around."

After Howard had gone, she turned to page three, on which
the *Post* traditionally lumped stories of accidents and crimes.
There it was, a short column on the right: "Two Negro
brothers from Spencerville"—but Spencerville was a large,
sprawling area; Judge Pugh's words: "You were determined
to satisfy your passionate desires in this vicious act. You are
not entitled to any consideration." "One of the brothers stared
stonily . . ." " 'I'm shocked,' said Stedman Prescott, Jr., lawyer
for the defendants. 'I'm going to appeal.' " "Trial of the third
Negro Joseph Johnson to be postponed . . ."

Mary Giles had never worked regularly for the Rosses and had
not come at all the past summer when the rape had taken
place. But she had been there yesterday, the very day of the
sentencing, working as doggedly as always—ironing, cleaning,
polishing—with never a word. But then she seldom said more
than "Yes, ma'am," always humble, always careful to keep her
place. Could these possibly be her sons?

There was only one way to know. The day was already full
for Frances Ross: a meeting at her church of the Social Action

33

Committee of which she was chairman; another later of the League of Women Voters; marketing; Christmas shopping and accumulated household chores to be done. Still, she would have to stop in at the bank where Mary Giles's husband worked, and where a teller had originally recommended Mary Giles as a good and faithful cleaning woman. That teller might know.

She dressed for the day as she did for almost any other: dark suit and light blouse. She was in her fifties, with sapphire blue eyes and white hair which she pulled smoothly back in a knot. She had a delicate, feminine, somewhat Victorian prettiness, and only her sharply chiseled profile gave a clue to the disciplined force that existed behind that cameo-like façade. ("Our greatest asset," said someone on the committee, later, "is that Frances Ross is so obviously respectable.")

"Yes, it is our Giles," said the teller, two hours later. "I'm so sorry for them. He's pathetic. He came in this morning and asked did we still want him to work here after his boys were sentenced."

"What a terrible thing we have done to them," said Mrs. Ross.

"I beg pardon?"

"Nothing. I was just thinking aloud, not about the Giles particularly. Well, I'll see what I can do to help."

She felt deeply disturbed to think that at no time during those months, which must have been so agonizing for Mary Giles, had she offered one word of comfort or hope; to realize that, however unintentionally, she had failed another human being.

"I could not let it rest," she explained later.

Once home that evening, she got the newspaper account again, looked up the telephone number of the defendants' lawyer, and called him to ask if she might ask him some questions. Was the death sentence for rape usual? Not necessarily; even in Maryland, the penalty began at eighteen months. What constituted rape? Well, it all hinged on the question of possible consent, and the degree of force. Had they terribly harmed the girl? Not at all. How could she find out about the trial? He would have the transcript before too long, and would let her read it.

On Friday of that week Mr. and Mrs. Giles brought, by prearrangement, a truckload of chicken manure. ("Howard Ross would never be happy without a garden.") They drove in the back, dumped their load in the long, low area that stretched far behind the house to tall evergreens, then returned to park in the driveway next to the house. Mrs. Giles stayed in the truck while her husband came to the back door for his check, deferential as always. Frances Ross was prepared for this. A coat over her shoulders, she ran out to the truck.

"Mary, I want you to come in. I've just found out about your boys. All this time I didn't know. I want to talk to you."

They came in and sat down, but talk proved almost useless with Mrs. Giles. She sat in a chair, her warm, rounded face a terrible gray-brown. Her hands lay open, palms up in her lap, and she wept so uncontrollably that it was hard to understand her words. "My John," she kept saying, "he won't be able to stand it. He'll die before they kill him. He can't stand being inside. All his life outdoors with animals—you know he tamed a raccoon when he was little, and wild rabbits." She could not drink the tea Mrs. Ross brought her and seemed almost unaware of the Christmas check thrust in her hand.

"They are not going to be killed," Frances Ross reiterated. "We'll do something. I promise you they won't be killed."

She had no idea how she would go about fulfilling that promise. But through Mary Giles's incoherence emerged one fact: on Monday night, after the sentencing, Reverend Mason had come to see them. He was the minister of the Methodist Church where they had both worked for thirteen years, Mr. Giles as janitor, Mary as cleaning woman. He had said he

35

would try to help them. Mrs. Ross knew him only slightly, but if he were concerned, perhaps he could enlist the concern of his church members; perhaps she, in turn, could enlist that of those in her church, and of others. Stedman Prescott had not had much hope for an appeal, so probably it would come down to asking the Governor for clemency. But how did you go about rolling up the snowball of public opinion until it reached such proportions that the Governor could not ignore a request for clemency?

She got the transcript, read it, and was horrified by the story it revealed. Hard to care about Mary Giles's sons, she thought, in that tawdry record, and she was glad she had never known them. Still, if you believed in the value of human life, it had to mean any human life. Also, if you believed in justice, you did not let yourself be deflected because the three young men involved in this case seemed as unappealing as the episode that July night had been sordid. She shared the transcript with Reverend Mason and with her own minister. Then, Christmas over and her daughters back at school, she began to roll the snowball.

All that spring she talked to any gathering willing to let her tell her story: church groups of all denominations, citizens' groups, women's clubs. Wherever a meeting was held Frances Ross appeared in her dark suit and light blouse, under her arm the large, expanding cardboard file where she kept her notes, to plead for the lives of the convicted rapists.

She had turned to both the local and national NAACP, which said they could not take on any legal defense because the case did not involve civil rights, but recommended the young white lawyer Hal Witt to assist Prescott in preparing an appeal. They also gave her a little money and promised support. The newly formed Montgomery County chapter of the American Civil Liberties Union did not have enough money at this point to give her any, but it remained interested and, when the case was carried to the Maryland Court of Appeals, wrote a brief as a "friend of the court."

Her strategy was now becoming clearer to her: to seek every legal remedy first. "And as long as we can keep it in the courts," said Hal Witt, "the boys will at least stay alive. And we can keep it going for some time, because Joe Johnson's trial, and appeal—when they come—will slow it up. They won't execute the Giles separately." If everything failed, then clemency remained. But the only sensible action was to prepare for a clemency appeal now.

She ended her speech before any group with a plea for sponsors; for volunteers who would speak to other groups; for anyone in the audience willing to take on the dull chores of typing, telephoning, addressing envelopes, and so on. She asked for money for mimeographing and the cost of carrying the case to the Appeals Court. And always she asked her listeners to write directly to the Governor asking for clemency, or to sign petitions. "The State House will file your letters and we'll hold your signatures until the time we are forced to go to the Governor."

Feeling that action in behalf of her sons might ease Mary Giles's burden, she took her along whenever possible, and always asked her to come to her house for the informal planning sessions she was now holding with the nucleus of a working committee she had gathered. Mary Giles's uncle, Caleb Adams, always "carried" her to these meetings because Mr. Giles worked at night and could never attend. Perhaps the meetings would not have helped him anyway. He continued in that state of stunned, apathetic silence he had shown when he came to her house the day after the sentencing.

"Mary Giles was more at ease around white people than he was. But they were both of a generation and background that couldn't understand demonstrations, or fighting for civil rights. And it never occurred to them that they had any personal rights. Up against the white world they were afraid to move in any direction; they were even afraid of going to the NAACP. 'The white judge might not like it,' Mary said to me."

Nor did the Giles have any idea *what* to do. A transcript of the preliminary hearing before the trial would have cost only thirty-five dollars, but they did not realize how such a transcript might be of crucial importance in time, nor did the lawyer they had managed to hire for that hearing explain the fact to them. When Mrs. Giles went to see him after that hearing about his defending her sons at the upcoming trial, he mentioned a sum which seemed to her so exorbitant that she rose, wordless, and left his office.

"Maybe we should have sold our house to get the money," she told Mrs. Ross. "I couldn't sell it. It's all we have and we both worked so hard to pay for it. We built it when the boys were little because we didn't want to live in the city. We wanted to be in a nice neighborhood. Always we've been good people, religious and not causing any trouble. My husband came from over in Howard County, but I've lived in this area all my life and my parents and grandparents before me. Besides, there are the other children; they need a home, too."

Frances Ross had come to know the Giles's house, now. It stood back from Batson Road in the sparsely settled area along the ridge. Red brick, it had a living room with a fireplace—walls covered with family photographs and religious mottoes—and three bedrooms on the ground floor. The full basement below had been turned into a recreation room, with one end partitioned off to make a bedroom for the boys. There John had built a runway for his dog to come to when it rained, and he was inclined to bring his snakes in there also. Behind the house remains of his activities were still visible: the wire-caged sheds

38

for his animals, the plot where he had had his garden. "He was in competition with my father on that garden," remembered Jacqueline Giles, who was seventeen at the time of the trial. "He was always trying to get his vegetables to come up sooner than the ones my father planted on his plot."

As far as Frances Ross could gather, religion was the center of Mrs. Giles's life. The tiny Baptist church up the road provided all the solace, joy, and social life she demanded. Every Sunday she forced all the children to go to both Sunday school and church. "My parents were old-fashioned," said Jacqueline. "When I joined the Girl Scouts, that was all new to Mother. James was good in athletics, and I was too, and I had my clubs. So we often had to stay after school and some teacher or other would have to drive us home. They were nice about it, but still . . . . Every once in a while I'd ask Mother wouldn't she learn to drive a car; it would have helped a lot. But she'd just laugh and say she was too old to learn to drive. And I sometimes wonder too, if things might have been different if father hadn't always worked at night . . . ."

What sort of people were the two brothers on Death Row? Could they have been "good boys, always good boys," as their mother kept insisting? It would be nice to believe they were, Frances Ross thought, and reassuring to have some other impression supplant the one left by the transcript of the trial. But risky.

She had written them almost as soon as she undertook to get their sentence commuted. Late in January a letter had come from John, thanking her for her interest, and protesting his innocence, on and on, in sentence after sentence, as though he could think of nothing else. Then came one from James, on the same ruled paper, with the same place for identifying number at the top (John was 7308 and James 7307), the same tiny red smudge affixed by the prison censor. James wrote:

I got special permission from my classification officer to send you this letter of thanks. I am very sorry do to the rules of the institution that I will not be able to write you again.

things are getting a little better here as time goes on. I am still trying to adjust to this sought of living. I try to read as much as possible I have found this the best way to past time we are confine to individual cells it's not a very big place it has ten cells each about 9x6 there are eight other inmates they are only people you see other than the officers the meals are fair nothing like you would have at home but they make up a balance diet.

Meager clues. If she could describe the brothers as people of basically good character, it would make her job of enlisting sympathy easier. She decided no. Instead she kept the issue abstract, limited to the injustice of an excessively severe sentence.

Even on an abstract level, the expanding file she carried with her constantly began to fill surprisingly fast with names, cards, pledges of help, and even checks.

V

Montgomery County is large, varied, beautiful. It straddles the northern triangle of the District of Columbia, and in the quiet years before the Second World War, most of the sections not close to Washington were still rural: farms and fruit orchards, estate and hunt country with white fences along the road, jumps for the horses sometimes visible, the houses rarely so. Artisans and shopkeepers lived in the slow-moving country towns on the fringes of which were Negro shacks. Or the Negroes lived in pockets of land, like the high ridge where the Giles and Johnson families lived, having the best of it with woods and the Patuxent River below them.

Rockville, where the first county courthouse was set up in 1777, held fewer than 1500 people in the 1940's, the "best" families living in the ample Victorian houses which lined Montgomery Avenue. Everyone knew everyone else and little except the political infighting of a county seat disturbed Rockville's relaxed tempo.

The war over and gasoline no longer rationed, that tempo accelerated with alarming speed. The lovely green land was up for grabs. The developers came, the bulldozers came, and out from Washington came six-lane highways to feed home-going civil servants into their split-levels, their high-risers, and later their "town houses." The Federal Government built its atomic energy plant and its Bureau of Standards near Rockville. Shopping centers, small industries, neon lights, car dumps, and used-car lots turned the old route of Rockville Pike into miles of squalid ugliness.

Throughout the fifties, party politics had less to do with how a voter cast his ballot than with which side of the conservative-liberal line he stood on, and for some years the county was caught in a political tug-of-war, first the liberals taking power and then the conservatives retrieving it.

When the county set up the Commission on Human Relations, the conservatives were mainly in control, and managed to sabotage its efforts. "We have no Negro problem," said two of its appointed members. Because of a small group of citizens, both white and black, thought there was a problem, and that worse would follow if action were not taken, a small group began to meet regularly, calling itself the Committee for Democratic Practices.

In that group, among others, Frances Ross found people who agreed to help her in her crusade in behalf of the Giles and Joe Johnson. Three of them she came to know well: Joe Forer, a lawyer, Alice Alt, and Jane Thayer. The two women took on the jobs of writing fact sheets, of working out the format of a petition for clemency, and of keeping card files on those people willing to sign petitions, help in any way, or give money. In time Joe Forer took on the defense of the boys.

Throughout the spring of 1962, the highly informal group constituting the Giles-Johnson Defense Committee evaded any publicity. "Not yet," had been the inhibiting advice of two lawyers. "Not while the case is pending in the courts."

It was Joe Forer who thought differently and prodded the committee into action.

"You must get it out," he insisted. "If you don't do it soon, those brothers will be dead. Give it every bit of publicity you can. For one thing, you're going to need all the money you can get, no matter which way the Court of Appeals rules. If they order a new trial, that will mean money. If they let the lower court decision stand, you'll need even more money, to take it to the Supreme Court. And that's what I think you're going to have to do. I'm willing to bet they let the lower court decision stand. I can't think for one minute the State of Maryland will be shocked by an instance of injustice."

The State of Maryland was not shocked. In July the Appeals Court upheld the verdict of the circuit court, and announced its decision just one day before the committee—taking Joe Forer's advice—held a large, open-to-the-public meeting. Among other results of that meeting, a small executive committee was duly empowered to continue the work.

That small committee met as needed at the Rosses' house in a development called Quaint Acres ("sounds like an appropriate address for a committee such as yours," someone scribbled across a petition for clemency which he returned unsigned). In the house only a Chinese screen separated the long living room from the dining area, so that when many people came all the space could be used. The whole effect of both rooms— four walls, rug, draperies—was of muted blue, accented by a few choice Chinese pieces.

There, some time after 8:00 in the evening, the Giles-Johnson Defense Committee would meet, once a month, once in several months, or—when the need for planning was acute —every night in the week. The members usually sat in the same places; Frances Ross occupied a low, straight chair at the doorway to the living room, notebook and pencil in hand. (She was a quiet chairman, who would start a meeting, let it out on a long leash—the while jotting down decisions all seemed to have agreed on—and then, having gauged the time left, including a coffee break, would pull in the leash to force the group to decide who would be responsible for what.)

Lewis Maddocks sat in an easy chair backed into the dining area. Round-faced, plump, middle-aged, glasses at his eyes, he was gifted with the ability to establish with anyone, almost at once, the kind of rapport which made conversation easy. He had taken his doctorate in Constitutional Law and taught it for fourteen years before joining the staff of the United Churches of Christ's Council for Christian Social Action. Before the first, publicized open meeting, he had neither read nor heard of the Giles.

"I just wandered in out of curiosity. Of course, the notice came to my office but I didn't go because of my job. Mainly I just wanted to know what this was all about. Then I asked so many questions—you know, what were the laws regarding rape in Maryland, and so on—that darned if they didn't make me vice-chairman of the executive committee."

Other men came to sit on the chairs at the dining end of the room. One was Reverend Mason, minister of the church which employed the senior Giles. He was a younger man than the new vice-chairman, Lew Maddocks, and a different type: lean, Lincolnesque profile, sensitive, controlled. Among the others were Roger Farquhar, a Quaker who edited the *Montgomery County Sentinel* and in time left the committee, feeling that his presence on it made him too partisan an editor; Roger Salem, who turned up often and put his public relations skills at the service of the committee; and John King, attorney and head of a church committee.

Howard Ross perched on the piano bench. An open hymnal was on the rack behind him. Sweet-faced, intelligent, he stayed in the background when it was his wife's show. Often he slipped out through the kitchen to go down for a final evening check on his garden or retreated to the study with a book. Though little given himself to the kinds of activities which engrossed his wife, he was completely in sympathy with her aims.

On the extra-length couch against the windows—or on folding chairs—were usually ranged the women who performed the time-consuming chores: Marion Merrill, a Unitarian like

44

several others, dug out and typed all the press reports at the Library of Congress (because she regularly typed material there for her history professor husband, she had space reserved for herself and her electric typewriter); Marie Ferington of the Friends' Meeting in the area, with her small, appealing face, took on any job handed her, including babysitting to free someone else to type; Greta Salem, Barbara Werber, Nancy Feldman, Rea Gleason, Hazel Pruitt, and a few others who did not come regularly. Jane Thayer was one of the most active. Just under forty, brown hair cut long, eyes thoughtful and manner grave, she had been recruited with Alice Alt from the Committee for Democratic Practices, and with Mrs. Alt handled publicity. (Two years later, when the three Thayer daughters were in school all day, she began work for a Ph.D. in Clinical Psychology and cut out her activity on the committee.)

Why were these tweed-suited suburban housewives sitting there in the first place? Not all of them were exclusively moved by pity and rage against injustice. One's guess might be that their interest had been caught originally by the publicity attendant on the rape case—perhaps so. Their motives were no doubt mixed. With some, political partisanship was a strong one. For the county's casual disposal of the Giles brothers (Joe Johnson had not yet been tried) was such a dramatic instance of the old-line courthouse attitude toward Negroes that a fight to save their lives became a fight against that attitude. Indeed, the "political types" on the committee were typical of various newcomers that the six-lane highways had brought to the county: attractive, articulate, as skilled in handling meetings as they were in running their households.

At the fireplace end of the room, beside Joe Forer, sat Hal Witt, suggested to help Stedman Prescott argue the case before the Appeals Court, and thereafter to carry on alone. He had grown up in New York, taken both undergraduate and law degrees at the University of Chicago, and was an idealistic intellectual. Just twenty-six, he felt that the logic of a case and telling precedents—which he was astute at digging up—should insure success. He had known Joe Forer all his life. Conversely, Forer, with only a daughter, had a paternal feeling about Witt, and when the older man became the main attorney for "the boys," the two worked well together: Forer seasoned and brilliant, practiced in handling judges and recalcitrant witnesses; Witt freshly briefed in legal scholarship.

There was no question whatsoever on which side of the liberal-conservative line Joe Forer stood; his entire legal career had gone into defending the underdog, even when his sympathies were not always with that underdog. The mask he wore was that of the wry, skeptical commentator, who—on the surface—seemed always to assume the worst of life and his fellowmen. Instead, actions refuting the public image he had shaped, he took on causes which often enough paid him next to nothing (like the Giles case), or were so unpopular that he risked his whole career in espousing them (like defending Communists in the McCarthy era). He could have put his exceptionally sharp legal mind to any number of lucrative legal pursuits. But cases which held—in Justice Holmes' words—"only the general pleasure of untying knots" were not for him.

Though at this stage, in the summer of 1962, he could not become legally involved in the Giles-Johnson case, he tried to come to the meetings, where he sat on a straight chair which he frequently tipped back against the hearth. He was just over fifty, of medium height, with close-cropped, graying hair and a figure as compact and agile as his mind, the result of a passion for tennis. His eyes were gray-blue, and laughter wrinkles spread from his temples. He had a slight lisp and, in the first few minutes of hearing him argue a case, you wondered why he had elected to plead law orally, rather than to bury himself with legal documents behind the scenes. Shortly you discovered the lisp was gone; you no longer even heard it.

Alice Alt completed the group, sunk in a deep-blue chair much too large for her to the right of the entrance to the living room. She did not fall into the category of the tweed-suited suburbanite. Of all the people in the room she was the most visibly and deeply impassioned on the subject which had brought them together: the death sentence for the Giles. With short, straight brown hair touched with gray, she wore glasses which did not obscure her luminous brown eyes. Always they revealed the intensity of her feelings. "Why must you lie awake nights about the Giles?" her brother had written her. "I think what you're doing is fine and I'm sending you a check, but need you get so involved?" It was a useless question. She was incapable of less than total involvement.

"If I don't seem loving," she said of herself, "it's because it's gone on too long." She was speaking of the Giles case specifically, but the remark revealed a kind of cosmic impatience. She was in a position to know. A student at the University of Vienna (from which both she and her husband had graduated), she had given all the pocket money she could command, in 1933, to help children whose parents were victims of the Nazis. In 1938 she and her husband Franz, a mathematician, writer, and computer expert, came as refugees to the United States, able to bring out with them some of her father's fine engravings and old, calfskin-bound books.

They lived in a little house where the bookcases reached the ceiling, those on one wall holding books in English, those on another books in other languages. When their daughter left for college and their son reached high school, she turned to work with the county NAACP and the Committee for Democratic Practices, where she met Joe Forer and Jane Thayer and responded to Frances Ross's appeal for help in the Giles-Johnson case.

In all it was a disparate group which came together in the Rosses' blue living room. It never became less disparate, but

47

it became more like a large family, whose members often bickered among themselves, but tolerated each other's differences. When the need for a detective became acute, for example, and no funds were readily available, Alice Alt lent some of the needed money, driving Frances Ross with her to draw it from a savings account.

"I don't understand what impels you to do this," said Frances Ross. "You say you are an agnostic."

"What is money for?" was Alice Alt's response.

There were differences between Alice Alt and Hal Witt, the young lawyer who believed in an intellectual approach and nonviolence. "I *don't* love my enemies," said Alice Alt, and more than once the two shouted at each other across the room, she wanting more action, he trusting to the merits of the case. The blowups occurred over peripheral matters.

"The *Washington Post* keeps calling them the 'three rapists,'" she said. "Hal, can't you stop it? People never read more than the headlines. They must change their language," and her voice became shrill.

"Why are you always attacking the *Post?*" he shouted back at her. "Just attacking people is not going to get us anywhere."

"It is true," she confessed afterward. "I do get angry at evil doings."

After Harold and Barbara Knapp joined the executive committee, they and the Forers met and became friends—indeed, more than friends. Between Harold and Joe it was a close, mutually affecting relationship: Harold (and Barbara) would prod Joe into some action he at first thought unnecessary; Joe, in turn, would curb Harold's impetuosity. Both Harold and Joe enjoyed exercising their wits on their interchanges.

"I'm concerned about Harold Knapp," Knapp commented at one meeting. (And with reason. He was by this time being sued for a million dollars by Stella Mae's family.) "I'm Harold Knapp's best friend."

"And his worst enemy," put in Joe Forer.

Jacqueline Giles Bishop came often to the meetings, always alert and interested, sometimes with her sister Sandra, sometimes with her husband. (Mrs. Ross had given her money for her training and she was now a secretary with a good job.) Mrs. Giles, too, came to many of the meetings, sitting quietly, alertly aware, although she seldom spoke.

"She would just sit there, hands in her lap, palms up," said Marie Ferington. "I had the feeling she was just enduring. Also, I felt those meetings must have been terribly hard on her. Here we were, talking plans and about collecting money and how many more signatures somebody had got, and of course there was nothing else we could do. She knew that, but still she must have wanted to scream at us, 'But those are my sons you are talking about!' "

Through Mrs. Giles the committee learned something of what life was like on Death Row. The family had not been permitted to see the brothers either the day of the sentencing or for the first month in the penitentiary. Thereafter they drove to Baltimore every Sunday, taking as many of the children as were at home. They drove over in Mr. Giles's truck in the early afternoon, parked as close as they could get to the gray, turreted building, and climbed the steps to its main entrance. There they waited, sometimes for a half hour, until a guard would admit them so that their credentials could be checked and they could be given a pass. Then they would come back down the steps, walk a block and a half around the massive wall which towered above them on their right, and be checked by more guards before they could go through the gate. Entrance was forbidden to anyone outside the immediate family. Often they had to wait almost an hour at this point, because only one family at a time was allowed on Death Row.

Inside were more steps through halls with iron grilles for walls, so that in no direction was vision blocked. When at last they reached the Row itself, a screened cage was moved first to the entrance to John's cell, then to James's. Behind that screen each member of the family would stand for a moment of constrained talk. Over their heads a TV set, placed so that each inmate might have a glimpse of it, blared continuously.

"Those trips were terrible for Mother," said Jackie. "Her heart was bad, and diabetes on top of that. All those steps. Then too, it would sometimes be so hot we could hardly breathe and we knew how much hotter it was in those tiny cells."

Early that June of 1962, before the Appeals Court had handed down its ruling, John was permitted to send his second letter to Mrs. Ross.

> I think doomed men rot in a [respectfully said] private hell while their cases are being appealed and they continue to rot after the death date is set. We live in the company of misery, not only our own but our neighbors we know very well that there are two roads out of death Row and it could be the one that leads to the gas chamber. One night on death row is too long and it would be hard on the imagination to tell what a long length of time would do to a person's mind because we are living in hope and fear and our mind is never very far off freedom or death.

VI

Almost instantly Joe Forer was proved to have been right when he said, "Get it out; give it publicity."

Announcement in the *Montgomery County Sentinel* of the general, open-to-the-public meeting in 1962 had two unexpected and important results. The first was a phone call.

"Mrs. Ross, I am Mrs. Donald Brooks, Dotty Brooks, and I read about your meeting and I thought I ought to call you. I don't know whether it will be any help or not . . ."

"We need any help we can get," said Mrs. Ross.

"Well, maybe I better explain first. My husband's adopted cousin, Tom Brooks, has been living with us for two years, while he went to high school in Hyattsville. He knows Stella Mae and William Rogers and all that crowd. The day after the thing happened—you know, on Batson Road—he read the report in the paper and he said, 'I know who that girl is. And nobody, black or white, should spend even one night in jail for having intercourse with her.' I'm ashamed that I never did anything about it right then, but I didn't know what to do, until I read about your committee."

"Would your cousin be willing to testify, do you think? Joe Johnson's trial—he's the third Negro—is coming up this September. Would your cousin at least be willing to talk to Joe's lawyer?"

"I'll talk him into it," said Dotty Brooks.

The second and, as it was to prove, vitally important result was a letter the *Sentinel* printed a week later (August 2, 1962) on its editorial page:

> Every time it comes clearly to my attention that someone is to be executed—be it Caryl Chessman or an unknown Hungarian sentenced to strangulation for opposing the state— I go through a certain amount of anguish. This is perhaps the result of having read Oscar Wilde's *Ballad of Reading Gaol* once too often. It's a childish reaction, but anyhow, I'm troubled.
>
> In the case of the young Giles brothers described in your editorial last week, there's a more substantive basis for concern. About the same time as these boys were sentenced, it was the duty of Judge Katherine Lawler Shook to impose sentence on Carl Estep, a very brutal rapist. Her reasoned sentence of life imprisonment instead of death was most carefully drawn. Judge Pugh's brief sentence of death for John and James Giles stands out in contrast.
>
> From studying the transcript of the trial, it seemed to me that the Giles brothers acted as well as rapists can, if that makes any sense. In spite of the repulsiveness of the offense, the motivation was simple, irresponsible passion, uncomplicated by brutality, and there appears to be some doubt that the older brother (22) is actually guilty. The 16-year-old victim submitted to her unhappy plight with no little calm and cooperation, and evidently survived the ordeal with as few aftereffects as possible.
>
> Why then the sentence of death by Judge Pugh and the declaration the court would show no mercy? The only way I can understand this is that his moral code must be very stern. He may have felt in this sentence, much as many conscientious judges before him at other times and places who meted out death to pickpockets and thieves, that the only way to stamp out unpardonable crime is to treat the perpetrators as severely as possible.
>
> Perhaps he is right and we are all the safer for his action.

Yet the sentence leaves me uncomfortable. I would hope that others would find the time to study the transcript and reach their own conclusions.

The letter was signed by Harold A. Knapp, Jr.

Mrs. Ross called Harold Knapp at once. Could he serve on the committee? Could he give some other kind of help? To both questions he answered "No." He explained that he was writing a lengthy report for the Atomic Energy Commission where he worked and would have to be in Nevada much of the fall. But he did have a suggestion: get some copies of the trial transcript made and distributed. He did not see how anybody could read that transcript, really read it, and think the brothers ought to be executed.

The committee liked the suggestion, borrowed the transcript again from Stedman Prescott, removed its staples, and distributed to any of the members able to type stencil paper and an allotment of pages. By August 30, the copies were finished —uneven, some with strikeovers, the product of some fifteen amateur typists, but legible. The committee placed them in the main Montgomery County library (the branches refused to house them) and in churches. No one gave any further thought to Harold Knapp.

They gave considerable thought, however, to Dotty Brooks's quotation from young Tom that no one should spend a night in jail for having intercourse with Stella Mae. Those words corroborated what they had not dared let themselves suspect: that Stella Mae's actions had not been those of a modest and virginal sixteen-year-old girl. "How could it be forcible rape," asked Alice Alt, "when she took off her clothes and folded them up—if she really did fold them, as the boys said?"

"To me," said Joe Forer, "what seems the strangest is the companionable, almost chatty way she told them she was going to have to claim rape."

To others, it seemed equally odd that when the two of them heard the approaching sirens, and James put on his clothes and fled, Stella Mae—knowing well that the police would soon find her—made no effort to put back on even one of those garments she had herself removed.

Tom Brooks's comment and their own suspicions induced the committee to hire a private detective to investigate whether or not there was substance to either. He had to work quickly because little time remained before Joe Johnson's trial in September. In one weekend he unearthed proof that William Rogers was given to fighting and to using obscene language; and that Stella Mae had been taken to juvenile court before the night on Batson Road for being "beyond the control of her parents."

The committee had no money for further investigations; nor did any of its members have any idea how they themselves could check into Stella's reputation. Alice Alt reported, after having looked into the matter, that the reputation of the girl in the famous Scottsboro rape case in the 1930's had been crucial to the judge's decision that the accused men were not guilty.* But Judge Pugh had allowed no comment on Stella's reputation in the Giles trial! And as to consent, what constituted consent on the part of any rape victim in Maryland?

It was hard to say. The Annotated Code (annotations were necessary since the basic penal code had been enacted in 1809) so hedged the word "consent" with loopholes that any lawyer with a reasonably agile mind could lead the jurors through at

---

* In the depression of the 1930's, nine Negro youths were bumming their way West in a freight car, in search of work. Two white girls were in the car with them, also bumming their way West. The youths were pulled off the train in Alabama. Shortly afterward, in Scottsboro, they were indicted for raping the two girls; eight of them received the death sentence. Public opinion and expert defense uncovered evidence of their innocence, but by the time they were released, some had been in jail for eleven years.

least one of them. The victim must "resist to the best of her ability unless overcome by numbers or threats," but "since resistance is necessarily relative, the presence or absence of it must depend on the facts and circumstances in each case."

"There is a wide difference," said the Code, "between consent and submission to the act of sexual intercourse. Consent may involve submission, but submission does not necessarily imply consent . . . . Force is an essential element of the crime of rape and, to justify a conviction, the evidence must warrant a conclusion either that the victim resisted and her resistance was overcome by force or that she was prevented from resisting by threats to her safety."

But, "Force may consist of threats without violence. Force may exist without violence. If the acts and threats of the defendant were reasonably calculated to create in the mind of the victim—having due regard to the circumstances in which she was placed—a real apprehension, due to fear, of imminent bodily harm, serious enough to impair or overcome her will to resist, then such acts and threats are the equivalent of force."†

Then came the matter of whether you could or could not believe the story of the victim. But on "credibility" the agents of justice in the Giles case had already reached their decision, succinctly stated by Judge Pugh in sentencing John: "Of course the jury didn't believe you; and the jury rightly didn't believe you."

On balance, the only workable decision for the committee seemed to be to forget about Stella Mae, let the lawyers work ahead on the legal front, and continue to seek publicity and petitions which Alice Alt was keeping in boxes shoved under a bed in the Alts' small, book-filled house until such time as the committee would appeal to the Governor for clemency. In

† Excerpts from Maryland Crimes and Offenses and Related Matters, *Maryland Annotated Code,* 1960 Supplement, Art. 27, Par. 461: Rape Generally.

the interim, the "boys" would stay alive as long as the lawyers could keep the case before the courts, and they went through the motions of asking the Appeals Court to reverse the lower court's decision.

The trial of Joe Johnson began on September 25, 1962, a year and two months after his arrest. It was held in another walnut-paneled room, this time in another county, in Annapolis. Though only one judge presided, two judges sat, and two Negroes were now on the jury. Joe's father, one of his sisters, the Giles family, and Caleb Adams were there. From the committee, only Frances Ross attended, arriving before Joe Johnson was brought in. She had never seen him before and felt a clutch at her heart as she looked at his small, thin face and his small, thin body, dwarfed by that of the bulky sheriff who escorted him. His attempt to smile at his father and sister showed half his front teeth missing. No "Tiger," she thought; more like a scared rabbit.

The court had appointed Victor Crawford and Robert Heeney to defend Joe. Heeney questioned him first, leading directly into his "General Discharge" from the Army (not stated at the trial were the actual reasons: unsuitable for further military service because of "character and behavior disorders" and "disruptive reactions to acute or special stress"). Next, knowing Kardy would ask if he did not, Heeney asked Joe if he had ever been convicted of a crime. He had. It was a fight with a friend; he had been convicted of assault, but had served no jail sentence. Next, Heeney led him through the story of that night on Batson Road, which Mrs. Ross had heard, read, helped to type, and discussed until she knew it by heart.

Leonard Kardy then got up, his round, boyish face still tanned from summer days outdoors. He stood half facing Joe, half facing the jurors, his resonant voice easily heard throughout the room.

Joe did not take Kardy's cross-examination meekly. The scared-rabbit look disappeared and he unleashed his "tiger" scrappiness. Beleaguered as he was, he shot his answers back promptly and was to be neither entrapped nor goaded into contradicting himself. "Do you mean to tell me and these gentlemen of the jury . . . ?" Kardy asked more than once, his voice mounting in incredulity. But that, on one subject or another, was precisely what Johnson meant to tell them.

Q. You deny that?
A. Yes, I do.
Q. Did Officer Collins make that up?
A. I don't know whether he made it up but I didn't say it.
Q. You didn't say it?
A. No, I didn't.
Q. Did you say, "James Giles then said let's get some pussy"?
A. No, I didn't.
Q. You deny that?
A. Yes, I do.
Q. And James said, "If you don't open the door I am going to fuck you up and your girl friend, too." Did you say that?
A. No, I didn't.
Q. You didn't say that either?
A. No.

. . . . .

Q. And you told the police that when you ran into the woods after the girl and John you had pussy on your mind, did you state that?
A. I did not.

. . . . .

Q. You told the police that, didn't you?
A. No, I didn't.
Q. You heard the police testify to that?
A. Yes, I did.
Q. You mean they were lying?

57

A.   They could have been. I am not saying they are lying but if they say I said it it's not true.

· · · · ·

Q.   When the Montgomery County police officers took their oath and told this Court and these Gentlemen of the Jury they weren't telling the truth . . . ?
A.   Not if they say that.
Q.   Well you heard them say it, didn't you?
A.   Could I stand up and object to it myself? I don't know law.
Q.   You heard them say it. You were seated here in the courtroom.
A.   Yeh, but by me hearing them say it can I get up my own self and tell them I didn't say that?

Two issues of that evening were critical: First, had the boys smashed the window because William Rogers had yelled insulting racial epithets at them, or because they had wanted the girl? With a conspiratorial glance at the jury, Kardy returned to that question.

Q.   All right, now you are telling this Court and the Gentlemen of the Jury when the three of you got back to the windows, standing outside that car in that dark, desolate wooded area in Montgomery County and with his windows rolled up he called you a black motherfucker again?
A.   Yes.
Q.   And what did you say?
A.   I asked him if he was man enough to get out of the car, how come he kept calling me names with the windows rolled up.

· · · · ·

Q.   You were ready to do battle?
A.   Well sometimes it helps.

The other issue of importance was whether Stella Mae had consented to intercourse or had been so terrified that she had submitted. When Joe and James found her in the woods, with John,

    Q.   Did you talk about having intercourse with her?
    A.   No, I did not. I said nothing to her about it.
    Q.   Why did you have intercourse with her?
    A.   What else was I supposed to do? To me at the time the way things were running it looked like she was willing.

· · · · ·

    Well, I'm not saying I hadn't done anything wrong, but well as far as sex relations with the girl I didn't figure that was wrong at the time.

Stella Mae, in a high-necked plaid dress, her hair hanging over her shoulders, appeared as pathetic and child-like as she had the year before. ("Think of your daughter," said Kardy to the jurors in his rebuttal, and later referred to Stella and William as "those two little children.")

On cross-examination Heeney reminded her that she had wanted John to lead her further into the woods, because she "would have a lot more chance to get away from one person than from three."

    Q.   I say, what did you tell him he could do when you went further into the woods?
    A.   I didn't tell him he could do anything.
    Q.   You didn't use the term he could have a little bit?
    A.   I may have said that.
    Q.   You did say that?
    A.   I may have.

But shortly she was saying she had said nothing to any of the three that night. "You didn't say a word to them?" "Not that I recall." Nor had she said anything to John except please not to call the others.

    Q.   And if he didn't call the other two boys you made a promise to him?

A. I made no promise to anyone. . . .
Q. Did you testify before you may have said he could have a little bit?
A. No, sir.
Q. You didn't testify to that a few minutes ago?
A. I possibly said it but I don't recall it definitely. . . .
Q. You didn't use the term, he could have a little bit?
A. I may have said that.
Q. You did say that?
A. I may have.

Thus it went. Consent or submission? At this trial she was asked for the first time whether she had told the boys—as they had reported—that she was going to claim rape.

Q. . . . Did you say to any of them, "I will tell you right now if I get caught with my clothes off I am screaming rape"?
A. No, sir.
Q. Did you ever tell any one of them that you were going to claim that they raped you?
A. Yes, sir.
Q. Who did you tell?
A. When they were leaving I said, "I am going to tell the police that I was raped."

Joe's other lawyer, Crawford, tried various tacks in cross-examining William Rogers. Didn't he have a pretty violent temper? (Objection. Sustained.) What did he know about Stella Mae's "general reputation in the community for chastity"? Finally he elicited the remark that William did know a few people "that knows her," but that he himself didn't know her reputation. Also, Crawford wanted Rogers to admit that if Stella Mae had opened the door on the woods side of the car and run into the woods, she could not possibly have seen William being hit by Joe on the other side. "Objection. He can't testify as to what somebody else could see."

Then came the defense's star witness: blond, slender Tom Brooks, in his early twenties like William Rogers, whom he had known most of his life. He was not frightened on the stand, but he had not wanted to be there in the first place and Dotty Brooks had had a real struggle to persuade him to testify. "You have to remember," she told him, "that there are two young men who care about living just as much as you do— and they're sentenced to death because nobody spoke out. Now maybe you can keep the third from being executed."

His ordeal seemed to consist of turning his head from Crawford to Kardy and from Kardy to the judges on the bench, as Crawford would start to ask a question, be interrupted by objections from Kardy, wait until the bench made its decision —almost invariably to sustain—and then start all over again with a slightly different phraseology cloaking the same question. In all there were three bench conferences ("I don't want an argument here in front of the jury," said the judge) with all the lawyers and the judges whispering to each other, while Tom, the jury, and the spectators all waited silently for the verdict.

At last Tom had a chance to speak:

> Q. Mr. Brooks, I will reask you this question. Have you heard her [Stella Mae's] reputation for chastity discussed in the neighborhood in which she lives?
> A. Yes, sir.
> Q. Is that reputation bad or is it good?
> A. Bad.

The defense rested. The State asked no further questions. The trial was over. It took the jury twenty-five minutes to reach the verdict of guilty. Then Joe Johnson was returned to Seven Locks jail to await his day of sentencing two months later.

VII

"Weren't you ever tempted to give the whole thing up?" a reporter asked Frances Ross.

"I suppose so," she answered, "but somehow it kept going of its own momentum. The lawyers always had a next step in mind and besides, things kept happening; it was like prying open Pandora's box a little bit at a time."

What happened in October of 1962, a week or so after the Johnson trial, was another telephone call from a stranger. This time the voice was that of a young girl, Evelyn Clark. She had dated William Rogers's brother for about a year and had been in the Rogers home the day after the "rape" episode. William had told her and his brother what had gone on and how he had cursed the Negroes. Would she be willing to sign an affidavit? She would.

So on that point at least, the boys had told the truth.

Young Hal Witt was now carrying on the defense of the Giles without pay, or with only such payment as the committee could manage from time to time. He thought Evelyn Clark's affidavit might be grounds for a new trial. His request was turned down because of Maryland's *Three-Day Rule:** a motion for a new trial on the basis of new evidence had to be filed within three days after the verdict.

* Largely because of the work of the committee, the rule was changed some years later.

Witt then asked the Appeals Court to reverse that decision and was, as expected, turned down. There remained now the Supreme Court.

Mrs. Ross had succeeded in getting herself placed on the Giles correspondence list, and in November she heard from James:

> On Tuesday of last week I got quite a shocking surprise when I saw our co-defendant (whose name we are not allowed to mention in letters) being brought to B-Dormitory (Death Row) and the startling impact lingers yet. Mother told me when she was here to visit Sunday the 18th that he was scheduled to be sentenced on the 20th, but somehow I had forgotten it right after the visit so I knew nothing of the sentencing . . . . Although he shows little outward emotions the effects of the sentence are deeply etched and understandably so; as I recall the first few days are all but unbearable and probably the most critical of all.

In December, approaching his second Christmas on Death Row, John Giles sent a card to Harold A. Knapp, Jr. For five months John had been treasuring that issue of the *Sentinel*—sent him by his family—which contained Knapp's letter on the severity of the sentence Pugh had handed out to the Giles. Christmas was the only time in the year when prisoners on Death Row might address mail to those not on their accepted list of correspondents. The prison authorities permitted nothing but a name to go on such greeting cards. So John had to send off his almost mute plea for communication hoping it would somehow touch the heart of the unknown writer of that letter.

VIII

When John's Christmas card arrived, Harold Knapp had been concentrating for several months, two of them in Nevada, on writing "Iodine 131 in Fresh Milk and Human Thyroids Following a Single Deposition of Nuclear Test Fallout." It had required an obsessive kind of attention; or he might have given it that kind of attention because that was his approach to any project he undertook.

Short, stocky, very blond—his Norwegian inheritance—he was nearing forty and was not immediately prepossessing. ("When he first came into my office," said Edward P. Morgan, the radio commentator, "I wondered why I had given him an appointment. Then he began talking and I decided I would listen to anything he said at any time.") A man of enormous mental and physical energy, he had never found a job which, confined to the normal working day, was enough to exhaust that energy. The completion of his "Iodine 131" study left him restless and in a state of vacuum. He was in that state when John's card arrived.

It puzzled him. The words "from John Gordon Giles" and the return address, 954 Forrest Street, Baltimore, meant nothing to him at first. Then, for he forgot few things, he remembered the brothers under death sentence for rape. He quickly sent a card in return which came back to him several weeks later marked "Not on prisoner's list of correspondents." Annoyed and affronted, he shot back a letter to the warden asking how he could get on John Giles's list. The reply was a form, with the particulars typed in:

> Dear Mr. Knapp, Jr.
> Name of Prisoner: John Gordon Giles
>> The above-named individual was sentenced December 11, 1961 in the *Montgomery County Circuit Court* to *BE EXECUTED* at this institution for *RAPE*.
>> We are making a study of each inmate in an effort to determine the best line of procedure in restoring him as a useful citizen. We ask that you honestly answer the following . . .
>> [How many times had Harold been arrested, how many times convicted, how many times in prison, which prisons, etc.]

Harold Knapp honestly answered, but he also indulged himself in the type of indiscretion which from time to time caused the penitentiary to take him off the prisoner's correspondence list: he put one circle around "restoring him as a useful citizen" and another around TO BE EXECUTED, drew a line connecting the two, and wrote OUCH! The warden did not appreciate it, but he did add Harold's name to John's list.

While this interchange was going on, Harold also decided to write the Governor for clemency. To his surprise, for he usually wrote quickly and with ease, he found it difficult to compose the letter. At last he spent all of a Saturday working at the task, only to find he still did not like what he had written.

"Then I decided that if I was going to interfere with the established and formally administered processes of justice, I had better know what I was doing and have a good, clear basis for doing it."

"He was only going to make a few inquiries," said his wife Barbara.

After thirteen years of marriage to the phenomenon that was her husband, she should have known what "a few inquiries" would inevitably lead to.

"Nobody would ever have heard of Harold Knapp," said Harold Knapp, who was given to talking of himself in the third person, "if Governor Dummer Academy in Newburyport, Massachusetts had not offered free tuition to some lad in the local high school."

His premise is debatable, but the fact remains that the Academy strongly influenced his interests. Having produced a flawless test in mathematics, he won the scholarship and entered a world different from what he had known. His father was a successful business man, "with some very restricted attitudes," said his son. "Virtue and success were as good as synonymous with him and he saw no basis for activities he thought would lead to neither. Like my spending a summer in Germany with the Experiment in International Living; or my sister's going to college. What was the point in college for a woman? Well, I went anyway, and so did she.

"What I got at the Academy, outside of my classes, he probably would have thought unacceptable. Math, science, athletics —those were all right; English—the Academy taught me to write; I'd always been scared to death to try to write anything, and I still can't spell—was all right, too. But my liking for German and music was beyond his understanding. Mother understood. She was the youngest of seven children in a Norwegian immigrant family, a very close family, and even when the children left home they still got together to sing. But the music I got at the Academy was on a different level: through my math teacher, who was a fine organist, and another who led the choir at Ipswich, which I joined."

The Academy was followed by M.I.T.—"in its grim way not a bad place; you get some things you just can't learn any-

66

place else."—He majored in mathematics with a minor in theoretical physics, writing his bachelor's thesis on Einstein's Theory of Relativity. Undergraduate work was interrupted by three years in the Army—"They were always sending me to take more courses, so I never got overseas"—then back to M.I.T. and the finishing in one year of all the requirements for his doctorate except the dissertation. In time, that too was finished and he emerged Dr. Knapp, and with his wife went to work in the Naval Operations Evaluations Group in Washington.

"But the best thing Harold Knapp ever did," he said, "was to marry Barbara Baldwin"; and as the committee members came to know the two of them, they agreed. "Only Barbara," they said, "could have put up with Harold's restless energy and drive for perfection."

She countered his pink blondness with dark eyes and short dark hair, worn brushed back. She was pretty—when excited, very pretty—with a rounded chin, even white teeth, and a strong, well-cut profile. She dressed with rare exceptions in a blouse and skirt, and gave, above all, an impression of integrity and intelligence. More nervous on the surface than Harold, she was likely to sputter when she got excited. "Harold, you've got to *do* something! Send a note to Joe Forer! Get his attention!" she kept whispering at one stage of a hearing on the Giles case. Or, at another, "Harold, we've *got* to find Joe and tell him . . ." But her basic self-control was strong, and broke only once during the peak of their activity for the Giles when she had had no more than four hours sleep several nights running; still—so did the self-control of everyone else connected with the enterprise!

Her father, a graduate student in forestry, had met and married Barbara's dark-eyed mother on a year's scholarship in Sweden. Their family life thereafter was spent in a tiny town in New Hampshire where he was Assistant State Forester.

The oldest of four children, Barbara went to a one-room school; her classmates were the children of itinerant lumbermen. By the time she was ready for high school her parents had decided that the local educational resources had been stretched as far as they could reasonably be expected to go. They sent Barbara to Northfield Academy, then to Wellesley College (with junior year at the University of Stockholm), where she majored in geology. Until the Knapps' first child Emily was born, Barbara worked for the Geological Survey in Washington.

This childhood background of isolation bred an unusual self-reliance, a skill on skis or in the water, and an ability to do any kind of sewing and to use almost any kind of tool. (When the Knapp family decided to become amateur radio operators, Barbara constructed the radio receiver, fitting together some 5000 parts. "You just follow directions," she said.) In short, her skills meshed well with Harold's and with the kind of life they wanted to live.

After Emily was born, the Knapps moved to a house in a small subdivision in Virginia, where the neighborhood association elected Harold head of the local civil defense committee (this was in the early '50's). Instead of paying lip service to the chore, he spent his evenings and weekends mapping the area, organizing the community for any eventuality, and studying all available material on atomic energy. Eventually he came up with a long article called *"South Woodley Looks at the H-Bomb."* It was published in the *Bulletin of Atomic Science* and resulted in his leaving his Naval Operations Job for one at the Atomic Energy Commission, newly located in the countryside near Rockville. So the Knapps (Gunnar was born two years after Emily) built a house on ten acres of land in a rural area of Montgomery County.

From the long driveway, which necessarily curved as it climbed to the top of the ridge, their house looked like a low brick box hugging the ground, for the lower story could not be seen from the entrance at the rear. Inside it combined practicality and charm. One wall of the dining room and the entire front wall of the living room were of glass, so that the light poured in, and from the inside one could sit and watch the ceaseless activities of the birds: red-headed woodpeckers, downy woodpeckers, and red-bellied sapsuckers pounding at the suet in an old red lantern hung from a slanted pole; the chickadees, wrens, and juncos in the ingeniously designed feeding boxes which Barbara had made and attached to the window ledges.

Barbara's work area opened off the kitchen, Harold's off the living room where he had his filing cabinets, a large desk, shelves of scientific books, and, hanging on the wall, the bugle which he used to summon the children from the woods. (In the early years on the ridge, Harold's filing cabinet and desk were full of material on land use—his extracurricular project being the preparation of documents on planning and zoning in Montgomery County—plus a bi-weekly column for a local newspaper on the same subject. Then planning files were replaced by those on Iodine 131, which gave way, in turn, to those on the Giles-Johnson case.)

Both inside and outside the house, the activities of all the Knapps (Christina, known as Tina, was born five years after Gunnar) were almost as ceaseless as those of the birds. Order and discipline shaped those activities. Blackboards, hanging on the dining room wall, were likely to carry a word list Emily was to learn that week, or a weekly algebraic problem for Gunnar to solve with the words "Papa will help" written beside it. In the kitchen affixed to the freezer were more lists, headed by the words "Papa's daily check list for everybody else." Each list included chores, exercises, piano practice, and always "Sing at night with papa."

Between the house and the other side of the ridge were a

basketball court with a shack beside it and a picnic table and benches which Harold had built. A target for archery practice was nearer the house. And hanging from one of the tall trees was a swing, to get to which the unwary victim of Harold's persuasion or challenge had to mount a ladder, as Harold later described to a newspaper reporter when that swing became famous because of the Giles-Johnson case:

"We showed them around, starting with the children's swing. We have a single chain swing, fastened to a branch of a tall oak tree, about forty feet above the ground on a sloping hill. A ladder, held up by chains from nearby trees, permits one to jump onto a wooden seat from a point about fifteen feet above the ground on the upper side of the hill. When the swing is on the other end of the arc, the person riding it is about thirty feet above the ground and about twice as high as the house. Few persons, except my children and me, think this is really their sport."

Music made up a part of every day, practicing for the children and singing at night; on weekends Harold frequently extricated himself from whichever extracurricular, or curricular, job occupied him to play Mozart or Bach for an hour. On summer evenings the family band (Barbara did not play) settled on the terrace, directly outside the glass-walled dining room, whose light illuminated their faces as though they were on stage: Emily, seated, banging soberly at the drums; Gunnar, cheeks distended, blowing one trumpet, Harold, another trumpet; and in front of them—taking her responsibilities the most seriously of all—Tina, conducting. The concatenation of sound was horrendous.

Other projects took up any conceivable slack. It might be the construction of removable bunks for an ordinary VW microbus, plus a small table-desk—not removable—for the space immediately behind the driver's seat, so that Harold could continue working while Barbara drove. Or it might be the construction of a flat-roofed, pagoda-like shelter Harold built for the eight children from the area who waited for the school bus down on the county road in the valley. It perched on stilts beside the stream which followed the road (John Giles wrote from prison: "I'd give anything in the world to fish in that stream, Mr. Knapp") and was surrounded by a railed deck. On the road side hung a plaque of wood with the words *Quercus magnae ex gladulis parvis* (great oaks from little acorns) cut into it.

Clearly none of this project-crammed life could have gone forward without the strongly developed sense of order and discipline which both Harold and Barbara shared. Nor could Harold have completed his projects without Barbara's supportive role. When he decided to write to the Governor asking clemency for the three Negroes and concluded he needed to inform himself more, it was Barbara who located a copy of the Giles trial transcript for him to read, with real study this time. When he remembered that Johnson, also, had now been tried, it was Barbara again who took on the chore of trying to get that transcript. No one, including the lawyer, thought anything different from the Giles case had come out of the Johnson trial, but Heeney said that he had a copy in his office and of course Barbara could come in and look at it.

"He loaned me a desk," she said, "and I had the impression he just expected me to flip through it for five minutes and then leave. But almost at once I found Tom Brooks's testimony; it didn't reveal much, but he did manage to say Stella Mae's reputation for chastity was bad. And there was William Rogers admitting his 'last conviction was for petty larceny,' and that was new. So I just sat there copying as fast as I could until they closed the office. When I brought my notes home and Harold read them that night, he was as excited as I was. So I called Heeney the next day and asked if I could come back.

"This time, after I'd been copying for a while, Heeney asked if I wanted to borrow it for the weekend. Of course I did. I typed out the vital parts all weekend. Sunday night, I remember, I typed almost all night. It's a long transcript. Then when I took it back he agreed that we could borrow it again. So we did. Then I realized I should have started at the beginning, so eventually I typed it all over again, on stencils, the whole thing this time."

It was the Johnson transcript that pushed Harold overboard. Here, in addition to other new and corroborative bits, Stella was admitting for the first time on cross-examination that she had told the Negroes she would claim rape.

Overboard for Harold meant total immersion. Once that point was reached, and the waters had closed over his head, his method of attack—whether the object was work-generated or something outside the office—was the same. It was based on two principles: First, you found out the problem, the real problem; next, you put everything related to that problem down on paper. "The man who really wins is the one who gets it all down on paper." The first problem in this case, he decided, was to find out what had *really* happened that night in July.

"Studied both transcripts for almost two hours," he wrote in a note to Hal Witt, now the sole defense attorney, since Prescott could not carry the case outside the state and it was soon to go to the Supreme Court. "From car to window smashing, concluded very complicated, at moment don't have foggiest notion what I think happened—or rather, still *very* confused."

He kept working ahead, as did Barbara, isolating key episodes and comparing the transcripts, finding contradictions in the testimony and contrasting what the Negroes said they had said on interrogation and what the testifying policeman claimed they had said, but had never shown them to read or sign. Soon he became less confused; the pieces of the puzzle began to fit. "It was like the theory of relativity; you started out thinking it was impossible, but the more you kept putting it all together, the more you realized that the incredible was the credible." At length he concluded that the Negroes had told the truth, and from then on his whole perspective changed.

"All that spring—or rather from April on, because I didn't really get started till then—I kept playing a dual role: that of analyst and that of detective, the first more than the second because there just wasn't enough time to follow out all the detective leads I wanted to. Nobody really had much hope of the outcome at the Supreme Court. Hal Witt based his appeal entirely on another vagary of the Maryland law: that the jury is the judge of the law as well as of the fact. Perfectly good point to base it on, all right, and there couldn't have been a more dramatic example of how fatal that system could be. Just look at the transcript: nobody ever told the jury what constituted rape as opposed to intercourse in the eyes of Maryland law. Nobody even mentioned the words 'reasonable doubt.' The jurors were told nothing, just plain nothing. But no one thought the Supreme Court would interfere with the State on that one. So we had to think in terms of clemency. My chief job, as I saw it, was to prepare a document for the Governor that would give him all the facts as far as anyone could get hold of them. In any time I had left over, I'd play detective."

He elected not to be on the committee, at that stage. "I just thought they were a bunch of do-gooders"—(it never occurred to him to apply that epithet to himself)—"and I'd be better off on my own. They were a real help, though, and Mrs. Ross gave me anything she had that might be useful. When I did follow leads, that report the private investigator had made so

73

many months before really gave me a head start. But at first, I was treated with a fair amount of legal scorn by the attorneys. They just thought, 'What the hell does this guy think he's doing?' "

Three months are a short time in which to compile a document as massive as the one he and Barbara produced: 127 mimeograph-length, single-spaced pages. Three months, however, proved to be the most he could hope for. On April 22, the Supreme Court turned down the case as "not federal," and Judge Pugh clearly would be setting the execution date. Letters spewed out from the Knapp household every night and multiplied over the weekends. Many of these went to John, who replied as often as the prison rules permitted.

> In answer to the Questions you sent I will answer them to the best of my knowledge. they are as follows below.
> No. 1. you ask what kind of fish we catch at the River and how big? we catch Sun perch, yellow perch, catfish, eel, blue gills. . . . I also catch "carp" but to me they are not very good eating. . . .

What he had done with the fish that night? "I left them there after this incident . . . because I was going to clean them on newspaper in Johnson's back yard." Where had they put their fishing tackle? Who had asked for the cigarette? Where had they put the lantern? The questions went on and on and John answered them all.

Harold put in every scrap of information he could get, whether it seemed relevant or not: a map blown-up in detail from the Geological Survey, on which he spotted the Giles and Johnson homes; another map he asked John to draw, showing area and paths. He included the fact that on that July night "the cloud cover at 2:00 A.M. EDT was 40 percent, and the visibility was 6 miles with haze"; the moon was nine degrees above the horizon at midnight and by 12:50 had dropped below the horizon. With Barbara and the children he drove to Batson Road in the daytime to photograph and measure distances, going again at night to confirm Kardy's description of "this lonely, desolate area." He put in isolated and key points from both trials. And on learning from Hal Witt what was the most authoritative work on the subject, he checked through the ten volumes of *Evidence in Trials at Common Law* to include pertinent quotations. Almost every page in the manuscript for the Governor carried a footnote; references were listed; there were thirteen appendices.

Among other matters he included as full a background as possible on the people involved. At that point he had little to go on concerning Stella Mae and William Rogers. But since he hoped to gather more when he turned from analyst to detective, and planned to make use of any detail that might serve to impugn their credibility as witnesses, it was the better part of persuasion and jurisprudence to do the same for the defendants.

No record existed on James, the younger brother. He had been in no trouble. At school he had been a popular student. (The committee gathered testimonial letters from his teachers, and the students at his last school, an integrated high school, signed a petition for clemency.) Joe Johnson's Army record "released to H. A. Knapp . . . upon presentation of a signed release from Johnson" was also put into the document: how he had gone AWOL "because I wanted to see my mother. She was in a mental institution," and his discharge because of "disruptive reactions to acute or special stress." His generally scrappy nature had also got him a fine and a record on the police books for "assault and battery." John supplied details of this in a letter to Harold, telling how Joe and his friend Thomas Johnson had got into a fight growing out of an argument. Thomas was sorry about it afterward, and came to Joe and "gave him the money he had payed for that fine. They got along nice after that."

John wrote of himself:

> altogether I have been picked up and charged by the police four times. the first time . . . I was in a Bar one night and got to much to drink, so I layed my head on a table in the Bar and went to sleep. and two police came by and took me to jail . . . and in truth I guess I was pretty drunk that time . . . the next time I was charged with something was . . . for hunting out of season, squirrel season in 1960 was from October the 15th. to the 31st. so on the first of November with out thinking about the date, I . . . shot two squirrels . . . the next time . . . was when I saw a man I knew driveing drunk, so I talked him into letting me drive him home, because . . . there was a very good chance of some one getting hurt. so on the way to his house a police stoped me and asked for my drivers license, I didn't have any, so they took us both to jail, him for being drunk, and me for no license . . . I still think I did more good in that case than bad. The other time I was charged with something was on that housebreaking charge, which you know about.

Harold knew only what John had written him and the brief account he himself got from the police records. John had been convicted of "housebreaking with intent to steal into the Spencerville Supply Company." What the owner said was missing were:

> 136 pennies
> 2 gallons white paint
> Sugar, coffee, other groceries.
> TOTAL VALUE $22.17

Not in time to use in the document for the Governor, Harold later got an affidavit from the son of the store owner, who was about John's age.

> I am especially well acquainted with John Giles. We were hunting companions for many years. John worked at the store, off and on, for me and my father for several years. The conditions of his employment were somewhat vague. John's greatest interest was in hunting and fishing and in taking care

76

of his animals. He worked just enough to satisfy his needs for cash . . . . I have never known what to think about the time the police caught John at the store very late at night with the same number of pennies (136) in his pocket as had been in the cash register. There were some groceries in a box out back which someone had taken from the store, and some white paint . . . . I don't think John would have had any use for these things. If he were involved, the groceries and paint would have to have been for someone else . . . . The police did chase after another car with its headlights out which came by soon after they saw John standing on the porch. They did not catch the car. I believe the man they suspected as the driver was killed in a fight before they ever had a chance to question him about the store incident. John had been working at the store that day. There was no sign of forceable entry, but the door was unlocked. The fact that he had the pennies in his pocket made him suspect, but I still have never known quite what to think about the incident.

It was for this "incident" that John was on probation at the time he met Stella Mae Watkins, who, he had testified, had said she also was on probation.

Meanwhile, the members of the committee were also working with the same driving sense of urgency. They were talking to people in the Baltimore area now, as well as to groups around Washington, and the signatures on the petitions for clemency had climbed into the thousands. *The Washington Post,* which in the beginning had been not so much hostile as indifferent, was now reporting the committee's activities with sympathy, and ran a 2,000-word story with pictures, called *Death Sentence in Rape Stirs Montgomery County Protest.* Other metropolitan papers and the local *Sentinel* reported favorably on what the committee was doing.

But another county paper was as vehement on the other side. Indeed, that side was not silent. It wrote letters to the newspapers complaining about "sob sisters and misguided do-gooders that always place the legal right of the hoodlum before all rights of the average citizen." Nor were all letters of appeal which the committee sent out returned with a contribution or even a signed petition. "Hell no. I'm no nigger lover," was written across one, and "Execute them as an example to all Niggers" across another.

By late May, the document for the Governor was in sufficiently final shape for Harold to turn to the role of detective, a reasonably simple one, he thought. It should require only that he follow out the leads in the detective's report and track down character witnesses. Then he would check leads implicit in the transcripts: either William Rogers was really a brawler and a "nigger-baiter" or he was not; either Stella had been on probation, or she had not. Both facts must be matters of public record, to be determined without too much difficulty. Full of confidence, he started his investigation.

IX

How does an ordinary citizen go about being a private detective? Harold decided that the process must bear some resemblance to scientific research: you guessed, pursued the guesses, and then—on the basis of what you found—either confirmed or contradicted the guess.

It was a good theory, but it did not work out well in practice. In any scientific research, he had always had time to let his mind play around the subject; now he had none. In his scientific field, he was familiar with the tools and knew his way around. Here, he most certainly did not know his way around, and again and again, in that floundering, beginning effort, he made false starts or wasted time on leads which proved unproductive. He was able to track down a few people who, although willing to tell him what they knew about either William or Stella, were obdurately unwilling to sign an affidavit, without which he could not begin to "impeach the credibility" of the two.

In the end, William Rogers proved easier to find out about than did Stella. The detective agency's report of the preceding September had included the facts that William had been arrested for "unlawful assembly" and "cursed, swore, was obscene, boisterous, loud and vulgar"—useful as leads, but not much more. Harold wrote to the police courts in the four neighboring suburbs; the replies were noncommittal. He tried to find William. Telephoning Rogerses' in Olney—the place William had said he lived, as reported in the Giles transcript—was a lengthy and futile procedure. He wrote to Tom Brooks: "Try Laurel," said Tom. Laurel, with its race track, had a large and floating population with as many Rogerses listed in the telephone directory as Olney had. Harold called Evelyn Clark, the girl who had given the affidavit: well, when she had been dating William's brother, the family had lived on Sandy Springs Road. He set out to find the address and when he came home that night put the results down in a memorandum:

> In Burtonsville, Maryland, I asked at the Fire Department where I could find the Rogers home. The fireman on duty said he'd heard the name but to ask the clerk in the grocery store, since he knew everybody in town.
>
> The clerk in the grocery store said that William Rogers was called "Red," that he hadn't been around for a couple of years and that his mother lived in the second house past the Hitching Post about 1¼ miles up the road.
>
> The waitress at the Hitching Post served me a hamburger and a cup of coffee. Asked if she could tell me where to find William Rogers. She said his mother lived just up the road, about 150 yards, but that William hadn't been around for years.
>
> I went on to the Rogers home to ask if anyone could tell me where to find William. A boy about 15 said he lived there but wasn't there now and to wait a minute. He called a girl about 20 who said Rogers wasn't there now. Asked where I could reach him. Was told he was now living at the White Horse Inn, Echo, New Jersey.
>
> Went to Laurel Police station (circa 7:15 P.M.) and asked the woman dispatcher if I could find out anything about William Rogers there. She said I'd have to speak to one of the policemen and called a car on the radio. Two officers came and I told them who I was looking for and why. They said I'd have to talk to the Corporal. Was told the Corporal would be by soon.

Shortly thereafter the Corporal came in. I told him my interest in William Rogers and asked if he had any record there. I was told I would have to ask the Chief about that, since they were not permitted to give out information in response to such inquiries. I asked if there was anything in the files which would make it worthwhile speaking to the chief. The Corporal looked at a card the dispatcher gave him out of the file and said "Yes."

Asked if he could suggest how I might learn about Rogers, or if he knew him or had any impression about him, his character and habits, the Corporal said he'd known Rogers for some time, he was a race track groom and a pool room shark, that it would be very difficult to find a permanent friend or a decent person who knew him, that everything he could say about Rogers would be derogatory, that he thought Rogers had been recently married that one place to make an inquiry was at the Maryland Racing Commission, Hagerstown, Maryland, that there was trouble every time Rogers came to town, that he had not only been in trouble himself, but had caused his younger brother to get in trouble too, that the police had tried to straighten him out and couldn't get anywhere and that if I wrote to the Chief he felt he'd give me information about the local record on William.

Harold wrote, and in time got a photostated copy of William's police record, which stopped in November, 1961. Seven of the counts were connected with careless or reckless driving; the others were "drinking on a Public Street, Disorderly Conduct by Fighting and Petty Larceny." None involved more than a fine.

William himself seemed to have vanished from the area and was not in the town of Echo, New Jersey—where the girl at his home had said she thought he was—because there was no Echo in the state. Harold combed the map. Atco seemed a good substitute. Harold put in a call to the keeper of wedding licenses in Atco, since William was supposed to be married now. No record. Then he guessed again and called the information operator in Atco: what plumbing outfits were listed in the town? William was a "plumber's helper" as well as a race-horse groom. Given the numbers of two, he telephoned one. "They said," he reported to Hal Witt, "that he wouldn't be back for an hour or so. So, apparently we have him." Having him, however, didn't mean much. William did not answer a letter sent in care of the plumbing outfit, and the police in Atco had no record on him. For the time being, Harold gave up the direct search for William.

Instead, he went to talk to Evelyn Clark in her mother's pleasant apartment, which, although not luxurious, revealed no hint of poverty. He found Evelyn attractive in a quiet, appealing, almost demure way, with her long hair piled high on her head. Her manners were socially correct. And yet? He kept wondering at the contrast between her appearance and the lack of hesitation with which she quoted William's profanity, at why she so freely offered an indictment of his character. Was it pique against William's brother, her former boyfriend, or a driving need for attention that would persuade an eighteen-year-old girl to place herself on record this way? In all such interviews he always talked in terms of the injustice that had been done; he talked movingly, but persuasion to the point of an affidavit was another matter. In Evelyn's case, she was willing to sign one for Harold, which proved to be much more damaging to William's testimony than the one she had signed for Hal Witt the year before.

So, as soon as he left her apartment, Harold sat in his car composing that affidavit. He had learned what was necessary from Hal Witt and was becoming skilled at restating words given him in an interview. (His files, alas, were filled with such affidavits which his interviewees, on second thought, had refused to sign.)

The affidavit read as follows:

AFFIDAVIT

STATE OF MARYLAND   )
COUNTY OF ANNE ARUNDEL), ss:

Evelyn Clark, being first duly sworn, deposes and says:

1. I am eighteen years of age, and reside at ――――― .

2. I am personally acquainted with William Rogers, of Olney and Laurel, Maryland, who was a principal witness for the prosecution in the cases of *State* v. *Giles* and *State* v. *Johnson.*

3. I used to date William Rogers's brother, Henry, regularly, for about a year.

4. William used to work at the race track in Laurel, Maryland.

5. William was quick-tempered, frequently in fights, occasionally carried a knife, and was extremely loud-mouthed, particularly after drinking. He cursed and used profanity profusely.

6. William on one occasion got into a fight with Robert Gooding, of Barbersville, Md. During the fight, William clawed Robert's face with a beer-can opener, so that Robert was in danger of losing an eye.

7. William was very prejudiced against colored people, and I have heard him use the expressions "black motherfucker" and "nigger."

8. William had a low opinion of the character for chastity of Stella Mae Watkins, and I have heard him say, "I think I'll go over to see Stella tonight and get a piece," and "I'm going over to see the whore from Hyattsville," referring to Stella.

9. William lived for several weeks in Laurel, Md., with a girl who had run away from home, and whom he later turned in to the police after he got tired of her.

/s/ Evelyn Clark

Subscribed and sworn to before me this 5 day of June, 1963.

/s/ Wm. H. Tipton

(SEAL)   Notary Public in and for the State of Maryland, A.A. Co.

Evelyn also gave Harold the name of someone else who might sign an affidavit. Harold telephoned him, explained his mission—it seemed to him he was now explaining it in his sleep—wrote out three pages of questions, and within two days had another affidavit, this time from a twenty-three-year-old engineer who had been a student in high school with William. Though more literate in tone than Evelyn's, it drew the same picture.

Harold now began to concentrate on Stella Mae. From the detective's report he knew she had been brought into the juvenile court of Prince George's County, where she lived, on two occasions: once when she was "out of parental control" and once when she was found "carrying a concealed weapon." The report had also given the name of one of her former boyfriends. Harold located him, found him quite as productive a source as Evelyn Clark had been—the ending of a "dating" relationship seemed to release acrimonious comment—but unwilling to sign anything: he was married now, and didn't want his wife to know of his connection with Stella. But he did supply the fact that he had heard she was married to a man named Livingston. They lived on such-and-such a street, and he worked in a gas station near her former home.

Harold salted that information away and began his attack on his real target: the juvenile courts of the county where she lived and in which the incident on Batson Road had taken place. At the Pentagon where he worked, he no longer ate in the cafeteria. Instead he took his lunch from home, washed his sandwiches down hastily with coffee from a thermos, and then—his pockets full of dimes—went down the hall to the public telephone. He could be seen sitting in the constricted space of that booth, day after day, a pad of paper on the ledge in front of him ready for the information which never came. It was the most frustrating period of any. He had originally

84

gone to see the Hyattsville police, only to learn that their records were automatically turned over to the county police. So daily he coaxed, badgered, begged, and pleaded with obdurate officials; calling juvenile court judges, detective bureaus, juvenile aids, precinct stations, probation and parole divisions of juvenile courts. His routine was to identify himself with extreme courtesy and state his mission and the reasons for his call. When he was given the runaround, or rebuked for presuming to inquire about the record of a juvenile, he would ask the person to call him if he thought of anything at all. He made several calls twice, hoping for a change of heart, and he followed them with letters.

Everyone connected with the case felt the same desperate urgency. The Supreme Court had turned it down late in April. At any moment Judge Pugh could be expected to set the execution date for the Giles, and that for Joe Johnson— once the Appellate Court had turned down his appeal, as was likely—would promptly follow. The committee redoubled its efforts to get signatures on petitions, staking its only hope on clemency from the Governor. Harold was staking his only hope on turning up new, exculpatory facts, and he was getting nowhere.

At this point Hal Witt called Harold to ask if he would make an effort to see Stella Mae and persuade her to talk to him, Hal Witt. He had called her with no success, but Harold might fare better. She just might be coaxed into writing a letter to the Governor, stating that although she had been through such a traumatic experience, she wished the three men no harm and earnestly requested clemency. Harold, he knew, had spoken to her at the start of his investigation and she had been pleasant, though adding nothing to her testimony at the trial.

Harold said he would try, and the consequences of doing

so made clear to him that the standards of behavior which functioned in the world he knew did not even exist in that of Stella Mae.

He went first to the place where she and her husband were supposed to live. No one there. He hesitated, and then on impulse decided to go to her parents' house: what could he lose but time? He drove his small VW to her street, slowing down till he spotted the bungalow with the right number. It was one of several formless little houses built around 1910, now on the fringes of a choicer subdivision area and not far from the dreariness of U.S. Route 1. He parked across the street, climbed the steps of the house, crossed the open porch, and knocked at the screen door. A thin, blond girl came to the other side, but did not open the door.

"Mrs. Livingston?"

No answer.

He tried again.

"I am Harold Knapp. I am looking for Stella Mae Watkins Livingston."

There was still no answer, merely a look on the other side of the screen of such fear and hatred as he had seldom seen on anyone's face. Then a woman's figure loomed up behind the girl and she began to scream at him, simultaneously pushing the screen door into his face until he had to retreat.

"What are you doing here? You get out! Get out this minute or I'll call the police!"

Harold retreated still further, trying vainly to explain who he was, that he meant no harm to anyone. His words did not interrupt the screaming woman, and before he had time to say more, he found himself suddenly assailed from the rear. A man—Stella's father? He had no time to wonder—had come up the steps behind him and before Harold could turn around, he was grabbed by the collar and the seat of his pants and dragged down onto the sidewalk.

"We want no nigger lovers around here. Don't you ever come near here again or we'll have you up for trespassing."

He vanished into the house and Harold could hear the inside door being slammed and bolted.

"I just stood there," he said. "I was so terribly mortified. Not because I'd been dragged down the steps, but because I'd muffed the whole thing. Now nobody would ever get to talk to Stella Mae; there wasn't a hope of getting a plea for clemency from her. And it was all my fault."

He drove around the corner and sat in the car, thinking. If he could apologize to someone close to Stella, if he could just explain . . .? Perhaps Livingston? He knew at which gas station he was supposed to be working. Again on impulse, he drove there. He left his car and approached a young man who was standing in an open space on the street side of the gasoline pumps. He had barely time for an inquiring "Mr. Livingston?" when a truck drove in, heading straight for him. He jumped out of the way. The truck stopped within ten feet of him and a fair-haired young man came at him with his fists up. Harold stepped back; the young man followed until he was almost on top of him, with the legs-apart stance of a storm trooper.

"I'm John Watkins of the D.C. police force," he said, and whipped his identification card out of his pocket to wave it in front of Harold's face. "If you say one more word to this man or to any member of my family, I'll cause real trouble for you. Go on, now. Get; fast."

Harold got. He was perturbed and shaken. When he reached home he called a superior of Watkins in the Metropolitan Police of Washington, wanting it to be a matter of record that one of his officers, out of uniform, had physically threatened Harold when he was trying to talk to another person. Then he went to his desk to write another letter to the judge of the Prince George's County juvenile court, to try yet once more to find out something about Stella Mae's record.

Two days later Judge Pugh set the execution date, notifying the warden of the penitentiary. A public announcement followed. It was to be July 8, less than three weeks hence.

On the day of the announcement Alice Alt and Jane Thayer drove to the Giles's house. Both parents were at home. They brought chairs out on the lawn and there the four of them sat through the long twilight of a June afternoon. Mr. Giles said nothing, his stocky figure slumped in his chair. Mrs. Giles sat as usual, with her hands lying on her lap, palms up. Her face looked ravaged. She went over the same story, again and again, how John had said to her, "Mother, I never touched her," and how James had said, "Yes, I was intimate with her, but she asked for it."

"Why would they tell me such things if they weren't true?"

Once, teen-agers in two cars drove slowly past on the road below, honking their horns and shouting "Get back into the trees, niggers," following that with boos and laughter. Mrs. Giles did not even look up. She lifted one hand in the direction of the road as though to brush away sounds that on this day were irrelevant and unimportant.

"I want to know exactly when," she repeated. "Is there any way you can find out when, what hour? I want to be near them when it happens. I don't want just to get word to come get their bodies."

"There was nothing I could do," said Alice Alt, later, "but put my arms around her and tell her 'Your boys are not going to be executed. I know. I promise you.' But that terrible tension never left her face."

The committee now dispatched its petitions with 5,000 signatures (keeping photostated copies) to the Governor, requesting him to halt the executions and hold a hearing. He consented to halt them, pending the outcome of Joe Johnson's appeal.

During this period Harold Knapp had a telephone call from the Prince George's County juvenile court. Requests for information such as he was seeking, he was told, had to come from the "attorney of record." Two minutes later Harold telephoned Stedman Prescott, Jr., since he had been the attorney at the Giles trial. "I'll write a memorandum for you of what I want to know about Stella Mae," said Harold, "and bring it to you tonight." The memorandum, like all of Harold's, was lengthy.

Prescott ignored the memorandum and wrote to the juvenile court judge asking only if he would be kind enough to investigate the existence of any parole, probation, or police records on Stella Mae Watkins.

A week later, Hal Witt called the juvenile court judge, and learned that what material had been uncovered had been sent directly to the Governor.

"May I see a copy?"

"No, but if you care to write to the Attorney General of Maryland in Annapolis, he may give you permission to see it."

Hal wrote. Permission was granted, and an appointment was made for him.

June was hot that year, so hot that almost everyone had left the offices in Annapolis by the time he got there. One clerk remained to hand him the file. He sat at a desk, his hand sticking damply to the pages as he copied the entire file. Then he thanked the clerk and drove back to Washington as fast as he could. He called Harold Knapp, started reading to him and was interrupted. "Wait a minute. Let me get Barbara on the other phone."

"Hi, Barbara," said Hal Witt when she came on. "Main thing is we've won. The governor can't possibly fail to give a complete pardon after he hears this. I'll just give you the main points. These are police and juvenile court records, both.

"April 14, 1961. Brought into juvenile court as being 'out of parental control.' Investigation officer thought 'she should be placed on probation and referred to the Mental Health Clinic.' So there we have her telling the boys that she was 'on probation,' though technically she was not.

"July 4, 1961, she called the police herself to say boys were coming to her house wanting her boyfriend to come out for a fight.

"July 20, 1961—well, no need to go into that one, the 'rape' on Batson Road.

"August 3, 1961, she was missing from home from 6:15 one day till 11:00 the next night, when the police found her at her mother's request and brought her home. Doesn't say anything about where she was.

"But here comes the real one and I won't try to read anything. I'll just tell you. This was August 26, just over a month from the time she claimed rape with Giles and Johnson. She went to a party in a man's apartment. There were about thirty men there, and I guess one other girl, but I'm not sure. Anyway, one man had intercourse with her in the bathroom 'against her will,' and another man on the lawn outside, when he had offered to take her home. That night, after she got home, she took thirty Bufferin tablets and some other pills, was taken to the Prince George's General Hospital and held there in the Psychiatric Ward for nine days. A friend came in to see her and she told him she had been raped by the two men. He, in turn, reported this to her parents and her father filed charges against the two men.

"The detective who was assigned to investigate interviewed her in the hospital and she told him that she had willingly had intercourse with the two men before, but that she didn't feel like it that night; that she'd often had intercourse with gangs of men and boys—there's the 'sixteen or seventeen this week and three more wouldn't make any difference' that the boys quoted at the trial, remember?—even when they were unknown to her, the detective quoted her as saying. And also she had indulged in oral sodomy with several boys.

"Think if the jury had heard that one!

"When she came out of the hospital, she was taken into the custody of the Montgomery County juvenile court. There was a hearing and Lieutenant Whelan, the one who supervised the interrogation of the Giles and Johnson in the police station after they were picked up, said that the State's Attorney—I suppose that's Kardy, though the report doesn't say—wanted her available as a State's witness in the trial and so she was sent to Montrose, that's a home for delinquent girls, 'not as a punishment,' the Court carefully explained to her, but 'for the help she could get there' and 'for her own protection.'

"In October, the order committing her to Montrose was rescinded, no reason given, and early in November she went back to high school for eleven days and then dropped out for the rest of the school year. Then there's the gun-carrying charge when a gun was thrown in the car she and James Fisher, 'a known delinquent,' were riding around in during a 'rumble.' The investigating officer in this case said he thought she and her parents should be required to attend the Mental Health Clinic; that the girl should be placed on probation, and also says 'the girl has a bad reputation in the neighborhood.' But all that was done about that one was that the petition was dismissed and the girl given a warning.

"That's all, except that she went back to school again for a while and then left before the end of her junior year."

"I suppose," said Barbara, "we ought to feel sorry for her."

"I'd feel sorrier for her," said Harold, "if she'd felt sorry at any point for the three boys."

There was scarcely time for the Knapps to write the boys in the penitentiary, in fact, there was no time at all. The already lengthy document they had prepared for the Governor had to be completely revised to incorporate the new evidence and to emphasize how the girl's history and words corroborated what the Giles and Joe Johnson had said of her actions and remarks.

"It was really frantic," said Barbara. "I kept trying to do six jobs at once. We'd learned that you couldn't send the Governor a mimeographed copy of anything—had to be an original—so after we'd done the revision, I typed the Governor's original and handed out the carbons to the people on the committee to stencil and I did some stenciling too. I remember how I typed right up to the last minute on the original and how Harold sort of grabbed the last page out of the typewriter and headed for Annapolis and the Governor's office. He got there just before the office closed.

"But of course that didn't end it. We still had to mimeograph the stencils and put those together. Various people had worked on the stenciling. It was a mess. They'd followed the carbons of what I'd done for the Governor, which was on regular typing paper, and the stencils were about a fifth longer so the page numbers went all haywire.

"You should have seen us that Saturday when we mimeographed it and put it all together. We met at a house the Friends had, next to their meeting house. It was the most conglomerate bunch of people conceivable: the committee, of course. The Giles sisters, Jacqueline and Sandra; Sandra was wearing her hair long then, like a red tower of Pisa, and I kept thinking it would fall down and get caught in the mimeograph machine. The Rosses were there with their two daughters who had brought some of their college friends, and Mrs. Ross had brought various elderly people, from her church, I guess. The whole Alt family was there: Teresa from Bryn Mawr and Jim still in high school. Mr. Alt had borrowed a big stapler from his office and Jim did the organizing—he's good at that kind of thing.

"So there we were with the mimeograph machine whacking away and pages thirty-two to thirty-eight laid out, say, on the kitchen sink, and fifty to fifty-six on a counter or on the top of the stove, and the rest of it spread out in batches on any level place we could find in the downstairs of that house. John Alt had all of us marching around in one continuous assembly line picking up the pages. Of course, people would pick up two of them by mistake. Mr. Alt was trying to keep out duplicates and do the stapling, but I must say the final product sometimes was a bit confused.

"Some of us had brought sandwiches, and when we saw how long we were going to have to be there, a few of the college contingent went out to bring in coffee and more sandwiches. It was late before we finished. Then Harold and I parceled out the delivering jobs: that was the first excursion of its kind, I remember. Afterward we got to know the route pretty well. We hand-carried the document—it was a long thick book, really—Harold and I with copies to the juvenile court judge for Montgomery County and his assistant, then to the home addresses of the key reporters of the Washington newspapers and the announcers on the radio stations. We'd done a shorter version, too, just a summary and conclusions, so certain people just got that. I don't know what time we got home, but it was terribly late and the Alts, who were taking copies to some of the sponsors, got home even later."

At the next open-to-the-public meeting, the Knapps were given an official vote of thanks and thereafter became members of the executive committee.

And the Governor agreed to hear the lawyers and a small representation from the committee in October.

X

There was a slight lull—comparatively speaking—until October. Activity continued, but at a less frantic pace. Almost 2,000 more signatures from Maryland residents and 1,500 more from people in D.C. were added to the 5,000 already sent to the Governor. Letters proliferated. They came, as Mrs. Ross was to say to the Governor, "from such distinguished citizens as Mr. Dean Acheson down to people who have never before written a letter to a public official, and from such organizations as political precinct clubs, ministerial and rabbinical associations, and the Board of Christian Social Concern of the Methodist Church in the Baltimore Annual Conference."

James V. Bennett, Director of U. S. Bureau of Prisons in the U. S. Department of Justice, wrote to the Governor pointing out that the death sentence for rape was diminishing and that rape was now a capital offense almost exclusively in the South, where eighty-nine percent of those receiving the death sentence were Negroes.

Harold Knapp may ultimately have been responsible for that letter. The Knapps had taken on the responsibility for publicity on the committee, since Jane Thayer now had to give full time to her doctorate. Late in the summer Harold had sent the massive report to each of the Montgomery County Council members, to Dean Rusk and to Piérre Salinger (who had the Justice Department review it and conclude that since it involved no violation of any federal criminal statute, only Maryland could resolve the case).

Harold also made the necessary arrangements to correspond with James Giles—Joe Johnson's turn was to come later—and was surprised at the fluency and ease with which James wrote, so different from John's early cramped, misspelled attempts to communicate with a stranger. He almost had the feeling, at first, that James was having someone else write for him; then he would come across a sentence such as "You see the only job I have felt was in landscaping," and he would feel better: James himself, all right. He also got permission to send small dictionaries to the brothers, and the wrong forms and misspellings came close to vanishing. James was as forthright in his letters as John was, though he did not labor the point of innocence for himself. "As it stands," he wrote, "we are here for a crime that was very definitely not committed . . . The wrong I am guilty of [assault and battery] and am willing to pay for, has been literally ignored."

John's letters at this stage were full of his fears as to what the Governor might do. "I would like to get out of the deathhouse as soon as possible, but not bad enough to go out by way of a life sentence and that's apparently what the Governor would give us, but I am far to familiar with people doing life to think it is useful or reliable for me. . . ."

As October 15, the date for the clemency hearing, drew near, public interest in the outcome heightened and was fed by increasing publicity. Early in the month Frances Ross, Hal Witt, and Harold Knapp were interviewed for an hour-long radio broadcast. (They were careful never to mention Stella Mae by name; nevertheless, a year later her family brought suit against the three of them for $3,000,000.) The story appeared in the *New York Times* and in newspapers in Baltimore, San Francisco, and of course Washington.

95

A Washington paper ran an account of the case in four installments, in one of which the journalist spoke of interviewing people who had been on the jury at the Giles trial. Harold had had no idea that a list of jurors was available or that it was legal for jurors to comment after a trial. But if a newspaper reporter could interview them, so could he, and possibly—this was his hope—get from them a letter asking clemency from the Governor.

He had one week left before the Governor's hearing in Annapolis.

"That was a terrific week," Barbara remembered. "Harold left every afternoon and reached home about the same time Emily got home from school. Poor Emily! She had to be baby-sitter for Tina and often enough cook for me as well, because we'd be out late, or as late as we thought those jurors would be up. Usually I stayed out in the car while Harold went in, but I had to go along because Harold's absolutely hopeless on finding places, even with a map."

The strategy was for Harold to ask permission to talk to the ex-juror, leave a copy of the report he and Barbara had prepared for the Governor, and return the next day with a letter the Knapps had written for the juror to sign.

One ex-juror was too sick to be seen; another said, "I make up my mind about something right then and there. Then I don't want to think about it again." The man who had been foreman did not wish to comment, but he said he was thankful people existed "who would write a report like that."

For those who were willing to help, the Knapps always wrote the letters for presentation to the Governor. "In the first place," said Barbara, "there just wasn't enough time to let them try to compose their own, and in the second, several just weren't letter-writing types. One was a day laborer, I guess, and obviously had trouble just signing his name. One other was just the opposite: well educated, and very suspicious.

He questioned everything that Harold said and when Harold got back out to the car that day he said to me, 'Well, there's one there's not a chance of getting.' The queer thing was that the man telephoned that very night: he'd read through the report and was terribly disturbed; he'd be glad to sign a letter.

"Harold would sit and talk to each one, then make notes, and when we got home we'd incorporate what they'd said in a letter. I'd type it up and the next day go back with it for them to sign. Sometimes I'd have to make three trips to find the person at home. The main thing was, every one of the five we did get said his verdict would have been different if he'd known all the facts about Stella.

"I was awfully nervous about Harold's talking to the jurors," said Barbara. "More than about anything else at any time I was afraid the ones who wouldn't cooperate might go to the State and complain about what we were doing . . . and even the cooperative ones! We almost fell over backward not to pressure them. Of course, we weren't doing anything wrong, but our doing it at all could so easily have been misinterpreted. All of them said things to us in talking that we would have loved to put down on paper, but we didn't let ourselves. For instance, one of them said, 'Oh, we knew the girl was lying, all right, but the boys admitted it, didn't they?'

"You just get the whole picture from what that man said, I think. They'd never heard a word about the difference between rape and intercourse, and no notion what the legal definition of rape was. That man was such a nice fellow, and willing to think about it once he knew the facts. He was one of the first we drove over to see, being 'up-county' and not too far from us. Still, he took a lot of hunting down; he lived on the edge of a small town, which progress hadn't hit yet, and had a store where he sold farm machinery. The house we thought was his, wasn't—it belonged to his son—and he lived in a far more substantial house across the field. Usually I'd wait in the car for

97

Harold, but that time, while he went to the big house, I sat and talked with the daughter-in-law in their bungalow. It was spotless, and she had her washing going in a machine on the glassed-in porch. She was pleasant. At first we just passed the time of day, but then she wanted to know more about why we were there and I told her the story of the case and she was interested. The next day when I went back with the letter, her father was sitting there, looking at TV and waiting for his lunch. He read the letter through very slowly, nodded his head, and signed."

The clemency hearing was to be on Tuesday morning. The Knapps succeeded in getting the last letter signed on Sunday afternoon, about the time the Baltimore NAACP was holding a prayer vigil on the steps of the beautiful, mellow, rose-colored brick State House in Annapolis where, in 1784, the Congress of the United States had signed the treaty ending the Revolutionary War.

The early morning of October 15, 1963, was lovely, with the air soft, traces of green still lying in the shaded fields, and the sun shining through a misted, autumnal haze. "Such a day as this," the committee members thought, "can't help but be a good omen." From their house high on the ridge the Knapps started early to drive to Annapolis, even before the children left for school. (A committee member had taken Tina for the day.) Mrs. Harold Ickes, one of the sponsors, but on this occasion a speaker for the American Civil Liberties Union, stopped early for Frances Ross, who was waiting for her in her three-piece blue knit suit, white hair smooth, under her arm the expanding file in which were the thousands of signatures which Alice Alt had triumphantly delivered to her the day before. The hearing was to be at 10:30 and Annapolis was at least an hour's drive.

Aside from the lawyers, these three were the only ones from the committee to go. (Barbara went with Harold, but stayed outside in the marble corridor during the two hours the hearing lasted.) The absence of most of the committee members was intentional: they thought a large delegation would look like pressure. Also, the Secretary of State had written, as far back as August, that "several hundred people have already requested to be heard, and had to be refused." A *cause célèbre* the case had certainly become, as more than one newspaper stated.

Still, as Frances Ross and Mrs. Ickes walked from their parked car to the State House, they were not prepared for the crowds already milling around in the street and on the steps, their numbers almost equaled by the State Troopers, "as though they expected a riot." Within the building, twenty newsmen were interviewing and taking notes, while radio reporters and TV cameramen were setting up their paraphernalia; crowds of both blacks and whites were standing in the corridors because no seats remained inside the largest room that the State House provided, and space for more folding chairs than had already been brought in did not exist.

It was a formal room this morning, filled with a tension not lessened by the dramatic entrance of Governor Tawes, flanked by the Attorney General and the Secretary of State of Maryland. Tawes made up in drama what he lacked in personal impressiveness. He was sixty-nine, short, his thin white hair plastered to his head, double chin spreading over his collar, and dark-rimmed glasses resting on his short, turned-up nose. His was a face designed to go with the genial chuckle, the good-humored slap on the back. When he felt threatened or resentful—as he obviously did now—geniality soured into petulance. "Hostile" was the word later employed by reporters. "You certainly felt a lack of sympathy," said Frances Ross.

The reporters for the defense led off. Next came Frances

Ross, who had hoped for a quiet, intimate talk with the Governor in which she would ad lib. Luckily she had typed out what she meant to say and now read it.

"I am Mrs. Howard Ross, Chairman of the Giles-Johnson Defense Committee. It is my duty and pleasure to lay before Your Excellency these 6,724 names of Maryland residents who desire clemency for John and James Giles and Joseph E. Johnson. I must point out that these petitions were signed before anyone knew of the information which came to light last summer as the result of Dr. Knapp's work.

"I would be very surprised," she went on, "if more than two or three of these 6,724 who sought clemency—when it still seemed the boys were guilty—did not agree that Dr. Knapp's new information made justice in this case require reduced sentences or pardon. What we now know casts more than 'reasonable doubt' on the story of the accusers and establishes reasonable probability that there was consent, in which case there is no rape . . . .

"No one will sign anything lightly which has to do with the judicial system. We could not stand on a street corner and get scores of signatures an hour on something like this. Each signature represents someone who had to understand the whole situation as far as it was known . . . .

"There seems to have been much folly, but no crime . . . . These young men are not degenerates, they are not habitual criminals, they are simply very normal young men who were subjected to several severe temptations on the night of July 20, 1961 . . . ."

She spoke not much longer, and concluded with reading from one of Joe Johnson's letters. Mrs. Ickes spoke next, pleading for better rules of evidence in Maryland, and then Harold Knapp talked of the new evidence and the five letters from the jurors.

"I thought there were only four," said Governor Tawes.

Harold handed him the five letters and finished his brief talk.

Obviously, Frances Ross and Harold realized with dismay, Governor Tawes had not read the report so arduously prepared for him. Hearing that the jury did not know of Stella's having been brought into juvenile court, he asked, "Why wasn't a probation officer summoned to testify?"

"It was denied us," answered Stedman Prescott, "because such an appearance would have involved records of the juvenile court."

"Why wasn't testimony as to her general reputation for chastity and immorality brought out at the trial?"

"There is difficulty," said Hal Witt, "in bringing such attributes out at a trial . . . people are reluctant to testify and besides, what you can present in court on this under Maryland law is very limited."

The Attorney General then commented that a pre-sentencing probation report would have brought out much of the new evidence about the girl, and was reminded by Witt that Judge Pugh had not asked for such a report.

"Well," said Tawes, "I have searched and been unable to find in Maryland judicial history an example of any such drastic commutation as you are asking for."

In *The New Republic* (October 26, 1963), Murray Kempton reported on the hearing, saying, in part:

> The ordinary ritual of mercy for the guilty was turning horridly into a trial of official Maryland. Governor Tawes struggled to turn it back. "You talk," he said to Witt, "about the reputation of the girl, but we have records of the reputation of these three men, 'Assault and battery, housebreaking and larceny,' " he read. Witt interposed that the latter two entries had been part of one count against one defendant, and that petty. The Governor went back to his sheet, " 'Hunting without a license, fined $17.50.' "

He mustered all the sovereign severity that years of torment had left him. "It appears they would have been much better off if they just went home". . . .

At the end the Governor asked if State's Attorney Kardy had anything to offer. He stood up, a large, unashamed young man in a silk suit and said that he had prosecuted these cases without fear or favor. "After hearing all these facts," he finished, "we have no objection to having you grant clemency as a result of the facts that have been presented to you." Yet not a solitary fact had been presented which the State's Attorney of Montgomery County did not know or would not have been able to find out before the trial. He had resources superior to Knapp's in every way—except pertinacity and interest in justice. Still, he stood there in the assured virtue of an open mind; Leonard Kardy had just discovered good will.

At the beginning of the hearing Tawes had said he hoped it would be over by noon, making a point of saying he "had to attend a civil rights panel in the afternoon." He was detained a half hour beyond.

The ruling was to have been given on October 23. Tawes delayed it a day "to do some final work on my official statement." When it came it was what had been feared by all who had been in the same room with him that day in Annapolis: commutation to life imprisonment. Among other comments in Tawes's statement were these:

> I do not review here the question of guilt or innocence for, in my considered opinion, the guilt of these three persons has been established through judicial processes. Therefore, my duty now is to review the nature of the punishment to be imposed . . . .
> While many cases engender intense public attention and sentiment, I cannot abdicate my responsibility as Chief Executive by rendering decisions based solely upon public pressure. Each case, whether it be widely publicized or not, must and will be decided upon its own merits. It is with this awareness that I have approached the heavy and lonely bur-

den of determining the disposition to be made in the present cases . . . .

There is a serious question in my mind that justice in this case demands the execution of these individuals and I am compelled to resolve this doubt by commuting the death penalty in each case. They have, however, by the perpetration of such a serious crime so early in life, demonstrated that they do constitute a menace and threat from which the public must be protected. Taking all of these factors into account, it is my considered judgment that in this instance, justice to all will be fulfilled by the commutation of the death sentence, in each case, to life imprisonment.

The *Washington Daily News* responded with front-page banner headlines:

> Governor Tawes Spares Condemned Trio
> Giles Brothers–Johnson
> GET LIFE TERMS

Mrs. Ross, on being interviewed, said, "I am appalled . . . . There was immorality here, but there is a difference between immorality and crime . . . . We are certainly not going to give up."

"This case is not over," Harold Knapp was quoted as saying. "It's hardly begun."

TAWES SPARES THREE RAPISTS' LIVES was the headline on the front page of the *Washington Post,* which ran an editorial the same day titled "Meager Mercy." The *Post* also sent one of its reporters to interview Stella Mae. He was refused admission to the house by Stella's father.

> As he was leaving he was seized by Stella's brother . . . a Prince George's County police private, and told he was under arrest for trespassing. The Hyattsville City police were summoned and [the reporter] was taken to the police substation where Elder Watkins swore out warrants charging him with trespassing and disorderly conduct.

Hal Witt went immediately to the penitentiary to tell the boys. They had already been told by the warden, receiving the news in silence. They moved out of the death house the next morning.

John wrote:

> Well the Governor gave us life today, in the name of Justice—so he says, but I don't think he knows what he is talking about, because as far as Justice is concerned—Stella Mae Watkins don't need it, and we sure didn't get it—so where did the Justice go?

The day before the decision, Mrs. Giles went into a state of shock and had to be taken into the hospital. It was many days before she had recovered enough to be told.

XI

Dotty Brooks was an expert bridge player, and on Tuesday night in November of 1963, she was driving into Washington through heavy rain to play in a Federal League Match.

Her mind was not on bridge. It was on an open meeting of the Giles-Johnson Defense Committee, which she remembered was going to be held on that night at a church in Montgomery County. She had received a notice a few days before.

She was not on the committee and never had been; nor, in fact, had she had any connection with the case for more than a year after she had persuaded young Tom—the adopted cousin of her husband—to testify at Joe Johnson's trial that Stella Mae's reputation for chastity was "bad." From that date on, all she had known about the fate of the three "boys" was what she had read in the newspapers or seen on television. Had that lawyer—oh yes, his name was Crawford—had he ever done anything with all the leads she had given him—the names of all that gang that Tom and Stella Mae and William Rogers used to run around with? Had he even told the committee about them?

"I ought to have gone to that meeting," she kept saying to herself as the rain poured down and the windshield wipers slapped back and forth. "I ought to have gone."

She was more than halfway into the city when she turned around, drove back home to Hyattsville, rifled through her desk

until she found the notice, and started out again to find the
church where the meeting was being held. She found more of
a crowd than she had expected, with radio reporters and TV
cameras recording the session. She slid into a back seat and
waited. She was not a shy person, but she had always been
afraid to speak to a large group, and tonight she saw not one
familiar face. When the reporters and cameramen had finished,
someone at the front—must be Mrs. Ross—asked if there was
any further business. Scared but determined, Dotty raised her
hand, stood up, and blurted out:

"Does anyone here know that William Rogers has twice
been charged with rape? Does anyone know how bad Stella's
reputation really is?"

Her questions broke up the meeting. A young man with
pencil and notebook ready came to where she stood in the
back of the room: "I'm Hal Witt, attorney for the Giles and
Johnson." Another man also came, older, with thinning blond
hair. He finally broke into Hal Witt's questioning: "May I have
your telephone number and call you tomorrow?"

"Well, you know what Harold's telephone calls are like,"
said Dotty later. "How very proper he is and how, for one step
forward in a conversation, he takes ten back, until all of a
sudden you realize you are absolutely caught in his web."

The call was followed at once by a letter:

> Dear Mrs. Brooks:
>   It hasn't taken me long after our phone call to realize you
> are in a position to crack this case wide open by simply help-
> ing to arrange for the collection of additional evidence and
> sworn depositions. This should be done, I think, with delib-
> erate speed, but more than anything else, carefully and thor-
> oughly (and quietly) . . . . What you could do right away
> is first study the enclosed materials, so you will have a feeling
> for what is important—the actual details—and then it will
> be possible to work more profitably and speedily. Note par-
> ticularly appendices 3, 4, and 5 of the main report.

Also, don't talk too much about the case until you have had a chance to act. It may take some careful planning and coaxing to get the crucial material . . . . It would help, after you have read the enclosed, if you could start making a list of names, addresses, dates, events, questions, etc., which you think I should check into . . . ."

Thus began a working alliance between the Knapps and Dotty that stretched over several months of intensive, exhausting, occasionally risky investigation, some of which proved productive and some of which—after weeks of coddling, wheedling, and appealing to conscience—resulted only in a final "No." The affidavit which Harold had so hopefully written out would then be lodged in the Knapps' files under "Other Possible Witnesses."

Dotty took on her chores with gusto. ("She always goes whole-hog," her husband said with resignation.) She was in her early forties, attractive, extroverted, relaxed, and almost instantly likable. Wearing casual, well-chosen clothes, a matching band holding back her blond hair, she gave an impression of such vigor and abundant health that it was clear why she had won as many golf trophies as her husband and sons. Also, like the others who came in so fortuitously to shape the lives of the Giles and Joe Johnson, she was fitted by circumstances and personality to play the role she assumed.

She had grown up in Ohio, married at nineteen, and was widowed four years later when her husband was killed in World War II. From then until she met Georgia-born Donald Brooks, she had occupied herself with bringing up her small son, with Junior Leagues and Red Cross work, bridge, and golf. After they were married they had come to Hyattsville, in Prince George's County, where Donald first worked for his uncle and then went into real estate insurance. The house they had bought was rambling, idiosyncratic—having been added on to at various times—and charming.

107

In Hyattsville they had adopted first a girl, slightly older than Dotty's son, next a boy; and then had had two sons of their own. The rambling house was always full of children of varying ages, plus their friends who were attracted by the Brookses' easy, casual hospitality. And Dotty herself always attracted those in trouble, or in need of advice from a responsive person.

Don's wealthy uncle and his wife, themselves parents of five adopted children, also turned to Dotty to take charge of children and servants when they were away on long trips. "I stayed out in Laurel again and again, and got to know well the whole motley crowd their adopted son Tom picked up. I don't know why, but Tom was a rebel from the time he was twelve, and he found his kind among the rebels around there. They'd all gather around the family swimming pool. From the start I was told, 'Keep William Rogers off the property if you can; he's a troublemaker.' It wasn't easy. He'd be in the neighborhood a lot, visiting his grandmother because his own family was at loose ends, kind of botched up. And Laurel itself had an effect on all those kids and on the neighborhood, being a race-track town. Lots of people boarded horses and oddballs drifted in for the trial racing—you know, the hangers-on with stable jobs (William was a groom for a while), and the gambling and numbers that go on in a place like that. Finally Don and I just decided we weren't going to stay in Laurel anymore: we'd babysit with Uncle Don's kids here when they went on trips, but we wouldn't go there. So John, Tom's older brother, and Tom got to think of our house as a second home, and then we took Tom in for two years while he finished high school. That's how I got to know the whole cruddy bunch.

"And I guess it was good for the Giles that I did know them. What Harold and I were after was anything that would impeach the credibility of either William or Stella, especially

Stella, of course. Every fact we could dig up would be useful at a new trial and someday, we figured, there would have to be a new trial, and we needed to be ready for it. So I'd get confidences out of this one or that one—I'm good at getting confidences, but no good at getting things down on paper; I left that to Harold—then I'd check out the stories as best I could. I'd have three or four here at a time, and then I'd talk to them on the phone, too. As soon as they finished talking, I'd run to the telephone and call Harold.

"I had to be real careful with Tom. He'd help me, but still, he'd had sex plenty of times with Stella, and it embarrassed him to be around when someone else was telling his similar experiences with her. I never approached William; I never wanted him to come to this house, but I went through other people, and all that time William sort of clammed up. But just the same he was drunk and boisterous and following the horses and leaving his wife and there was never a time when you could put your finger on him. But he knew about what I was doing, and I'd hear through other people how he said 'I'm going to come down and get that dumb, blond cousin of Tom's sometime.'

"I could level with all of them about Stella and the rumbles and the gang-bangs. When Harold wasn't around, I'd just talk their language. After all, I didn't grow up with four brothers and have two husbands for nothing. I used four-letter words I hadn't thought of for years, but they came in handy. I'd say, 'Now, let's call a spade a spade. I don't give a damn what you say and I don't want you to give a damn what I say,' and I'd sling out the old four-letter words and you could almost see them relax. But even I was shocked with the stuff that came out. And Don was worried. His patience was almost exhausted the way they'd drop in here any hour of the night. Besides, he was scared I couldn't handle them. I knew I could, but he didn't. Still, there wasn't a moment when he didn't have full respect for Harold and what he was trying to do for those boys. Pretty good for a Georgia boy, yes?"

Through November and early December, each step seemed to turn up fresh corroboration of the testimony of the Negroes. "The bulk of it came from the people I first bumped into. I can honestly say that one thing led to another. Somebody'd mention three names. I'd call to get in touch with them. Then one of them would mention two others. Finding their telephone numbers or tracking down where they worked or where they lived—most of them didn't have telephones at home—well, that took hours. Then I'd try to get their stories. Always Harold kept cautioning me, 'Don't get them to say things you want to hear. Be extremely cautious.' And he'd send me five-page letters telling me how to act and what to say. Believe me, Harold's a hard taskmaster: it wasn't anything he said, he's too polite for that; but I knew if I didn't get the stuff he asked for, I'd feel like a heel the next time I saw him.

"And believe me, that gang wasn't above asking for handouts. Not right out, but one would say, for instance, on the telephone, that he couldn't get over that night because—well, usually it was something connected with his car, a bad tire, or a part that needed replacing, or stuff like that. He'd be glad to come, only he didn't have the money to get the car fixed. At that stage I didn't care. I'd say, 'O.K. I'll pay for the tire or whatever, but you get over here!' It wasn't only that one. All that crowd, the girls too, were cadgers: I'd meet this one at the grocery store to buy milk for her baby, and that one on a corner to give her money for God knows what! Never much, but you get the picture. All I cared about was to have them talk. And they sure talked. Then the second they left I'd run to the phone to call Harold. Then he'd follow up with those letters of his. He always wanted them to understand the whole case, before he tried to get them to sign an affidavit. He was famous for those letters."

Rightly famous, one would have decided, struggling through one of those six- or seven-page, single-spaced ("and Barbara-typed") letters. The format, the words chosen, were so far above the mental level of many of the recipients that it would have seemed they could only fail of their purpose. With the more literate, this suspicion often proved justified: they looked at the dense pages, glanced at the documents and reports Harold attached, and frequently gave up.

With the group Dotty and Harold were dealing with, the opposite was true: they were flattered. Elston, the twenty-seven-year-old barber; the TV repair man now espousing his wife's Seventh-day Adventist views on morals and meat-eating, the twenty-year-old in the Army; various others, including Tom Brooks, all were flattered at being treated—probably for the first time in their lives—as intellectuals who, that man Harold Knapp seemed to assume, were capable of digesting and understanding the mass of material he sent them. They were disconcerted, but equally flattered, by Harold's almost old-world politeness of manner when they met him.

Thus, the combination of Dotty's breezy, Midwestern manner and Harold's precision and courteousness at times paid off. One morning, during a blizzard, they converged on the house of Tom's older brother and there got three affidavits and snared two people who agreed that they would be willing to testify on the stand. But of course they were not content with these results.

Dotty, using a cross-directory of everyone in the area where Stella lived—and, as it happened, not far from where the Brookses themselves lived—hunted through the names to see whether she knew any of their owners. "And that's how I found Genevieve. I guess I'd known her at the country club, or through politics—I once managed a campaign for a Republican candidate—and I found she lived pretty close to the Watkinses and knew all the scuttlebutt about the family. I'd call her five times a week with questions and believe me, if I didn't, I'd get a call from Harold. He kept saying we'd have to check out what she said; you know, neighbors can be pretty malicious. But it all proved. When he was prosecuting, Kardy more than implied that Stella had had to be put in the Home for Delinquent Girls for her own protection, and so did her mother on the stand: on account of the publicity from the rape, all the boys kept hounding her, they both implied. But that wasn't Genevieve's story: according to her the boys had been turning the neighborhood into a red-light district long before that night on Batson Road. The Watkinses had called the police plenty of times and Stella even had herself.

"One night the police were supposed to have arrested seventeen boys hanging around her house, so Harold put me to checking their records at the courthouse. That's the way Harold is. If somebody gave him a puzzle of a thousand pieces, and one piece got lost between his house and that of the giver, he'd never stop till he found that one piece.

"I spent so much time digging around the records here in Prince George's County that our lawyer friends would spot me and come around and say, 'What the hell are you doing here, Dotty? Don't you know you're associating with a Red group? Don't you know you're going to get a shot in the head one of these nights?' And in just little ways, moving socially and stuff, I was always being told what an idiot I was to be involved with 'three niggers in jail and if the state would burn 6000 of them it wouldn't be enough.'

"I guess I was lucky to get by with all I was doing. There was the night I spent talking to Jane Clemens and her mother, Mrs. Rodney. Jane's the one about whom it was said that at the gang-bangs 'Jane just watched.' Hmmm . . . . In the end, and after all those months of working on her, she wouldn't sign an affidavit. I did everything I could. Why, one night I even pretended I was drunk. We sat around the kitchen and Jane's mother just poured drink after drink for herself and Jane. The mother admitted things about Stella, and then she'd say, 'But she needed a mother. She'd come in here and say "Hi, Mom." ' So I said to Mrs. Rodney, 'I wish I could truthfully come in here and say I was the chairman of a committee to send Stella to college, or buy her a house or give her good things, but unfortunately she sent three men to Death Row and we've got to think about everyone's life.' And of course I'd get, 'Yes, you'd let three niggers run loose and bother one poor little white girl.' That was one of the nights that I got home and found Don pacing the floor. I'd left something like 8:00 and didn't get home till 1:30.

"Then there were other neighbors I went to see, and one of them said she was going to sue me . . . gee, then I got home and got sick at my stomach and so scared for my kids and I called Harold and said, 'Could I have a lawsuit on my hands?'

"Mrs. Rodney, Jane's mother, thought I ought to be sued, too, and there was another woman. When I was checking out those seventeen boys who were arrested for molesting Stella, I called one of them direct and his mother got wind of it and she called me one night and said she'd got a lawyer and the papers would be served on me right away. I know I didn't say more than eight words and she talked for two and a half hours and my husband paced the floor and he kept saying, 'Hang up! Now you hang up.' So I finally did and she called right back.

"Somehow, I got by with it all. It was a very, very exciting time."

For Harold, the time was not so much exciting as it was exhausting, characteristized by an unflagging and dogged pursuit, through the course of which he came close to collapse from lack of sleep. And although he might have talked to

Dotty three times a day on the telephone, or stopped by to see her in person, he would have another idea when he was ready to go to bed, or a new name he had picked up during the course of the evening as he talked, say, to the owner of the Pizza Palace, which Stella was said to frequent, or the Florida Inn where she had sung as an entertainer. So he would write Dotty a note: "If you have any chance to find out about, or talk to, or learn the whereabouts of one ———." Or, "One added thought. In a gentle way find out what relation Tim Calloway, Stella's ex-boyfriend, had with Tom and all the others . . . . He knows a lot more than he's told so far." Or, "I'm still looking for:

"Glen Wykoff, aged 32—alleged raper of Stella at party after which she took sleeping pills.

"Arthur Jones, 30—other alleged raper.

"Leslie Barons—reported alleged rapes to Stella's parents.

"Hubert McIntyre, aged 40, at whose house alleged rape and party occurred.

"I find McIntyre has skipped town, leaving a lot of debts— Stella knows such nice people. But I can't seem to track down the others."

(Glen Wykoff was not tracked down until a year later when, by a quirk of fate, he was discovered to be in the Baltimore Penitentiary, serving a life sentence for murder. There he produced an affidavit which James Giles forwarded to Harold!)

Of everyone, Harold asked, and in turn asked Dotty to ask, whether Stella had had relations with Negroes before the night on Batson Road, a question which seemed unwarranted at the time, but which proved to be the first one Justice Black asked in the Supreme Court. Always there were rumors, but no proof. Harold worked on Mark White, who had driven Stella and William to the Rock that evening, and then left them to get gas. He signed an affidavit that he had not taken his bathing suit with him; the police found none in the car. The quest for that affidavit also seemed unimportant, but a judge later found it relevant.

Harold also pursued William Rogers, by letters—to the race track in Laurel, to the police in any place he was known to have stayed, to former employers—one netting, in April, the fact that William was held on a bastardy charge in New Jersey. Finally he pursued William in person, for toward summer William was known to be back in the area. Harold spent one evening with him at a tavern, and another night succeeded in getting him and a friend to come to his house. He had written an affidavit for him to sign and had it waiting. It was never used. Harold's tactics at this stage were to try to make a friend of William, and then, friendship achieved, wheedle him into signing the affidavit. The tactics proved unavailing.

The planning and the letters were incessant:

General Orders #1

H.q. Germantown Theater Command
March 20, 1964

To: B. Knapp
     D. Brooks

From: H. Knapp

Subject: Orders of the Day

1. B. Knapp proceed to Hyattsville to join forces with D. Brooks.
2. Proceed to Upper Marlboro. D. Brooks read and get briefed by B. Knapp en route and v.v. [vice versa]
3. Check the docket (or whatever it is they call the record of cases which come before the Court) for . . . . Be alert to anything ———— . If the process of looking over the day-by-day cases isn't too formidable, check to see if Watkins had anything scheduled in June to September, 1961. Copy down whatever you find that is pertinent. It may be

the search will lead back to Hyattsville People's Court . . . .

4. Before leaving Upper Marlboro, go see Judge Loveless and tell him ———— and ask him ————.

5. If you dare, go to Senate Inn and inquire about Mrs. Watkins.

6. If you have time, go to Seat Pleasant police station to the Juvenile Squad downstairs and talk to Lt. Kerns and lady officer Polly re Stella when picked up by them . . . . also Kerns may know about 21 boys and rape, lots else . . . .

As if such extracurricular activities were not enough, Harold contrived to put out a brief, lucid newsletter on the history of the case to date; he also worked ahead on what was to be known as the Blue Report, kept the letters going to the penitentiary, and went to see the three for the first time. He saw John and James once again, when late in March they were brought handcuffed in a black van from Baltimore to see briefly the body of their forty-eight-year-old mother, as it lay in the Round Oak Baptist Church, awaiting the funeral service for which the brothers were not allowed to stay.

XII

Before Dotty went to interview a girl who had been to parties with Stella Mae, Harold's instructions included: "Tell her not to be shy about what she says. Tell her that by now we've heard everything."

So they had. "Everything" had come from some thirty young people, only a handful of whom were willing to go on public record, but all of whom were willing to tell what they knew—in confidence. They seemed to exist in a spiritual vacuum which they tried to fill with physical excitement: variety in sexual partners, petty thievery, brushes with the law. The men moved from job to job, from one rooming house or apartment to another, leaving a trail of unpaid debts behind. The girls moved from man to man, or casually married the one momentarily preferred. (One, for example, had been caught stealing along with her husband, but did not share his prison sentence because she was pregnant. "I was sorry the baby died," she later told Dotty, "because my mother thought I ought to get a job.") The girls were pretty, dressed modestly, and had better manners than the men. But all seemed to lack any sense of personal worth, a rootless, goal-less, identity-less group, coming almost always from broken homes or homes in which one or the other parent was an alcoholic, but not from a background of real poverty.

And the eye of the storm, Stella herself?

The picture had necessarily to be pieced together from police and juvenile court records, and from impressions and comments of those who knew her. For, until the summer of 1964, only Mrs. Ross had seen her, as she had sat in the witness box at Joe Johnson's trial: wan, composed, and pathetic to look at.

"This is the case of a tall, thin girl who apparently has been allowed to do as she pleases until her mother began to worry about her being completely beyond control," wrote a parole officer who was sent to investigate the situation when Stella Mae was in the tenth grade and had just turned sixteen—three months before the episode on Batson Road.

Mrs. Watkins had herself initiated that first investigation, by making a formal petition to the juvenile court of Prince George's County "to make such findings and pass such order of Decree as the law provides." The reason officially stated was that "the subject was beyond the control of her parents, and keeping late hours." And "the subject concurs in above version," added the report.

The investigator described the family: the father twenty years older than the mother, a regular drinker, with a sixth-grade education and a humble job, not a churchgoer, although his wife (with a tenth-grade education) went regularly. There were four children, a girl eight years older than Stella, long since married and living in the West, and two sons, shortly to become policemen. Stella was the youngest.

"Neither parent agrees on the way to control this subject," the report went on. "Her mother has never allowed her to do any housework or have any responsibility in the home. The father feels that she should be given certain responsibilities and made to obey certain rules of behavior. Her mother feels she is old-fashioned and maybe she is too strict and that she does not want the girl to feel she must be forced into going to church and associating with the right friends. The subject readily admits slipping out and meeting boys after the family goes to bed and keeps late hours." (In the preceding fall, Stella was picked up for disturbing the peace, but never charged; a month later the police were again involved with Stella, when her mother called them to say that Stella had left home at 1:50 A.M. after an argument with her.) "She picks her friends from children who have been in trouble with the law and girls whose parents have no control over them."

The subject also was "emotionally unstable" and had health problems on which the parole officer based her *Summary:* "It is the opinion of the investigating officer that this girl should be placed on probation, and referred to the Mental Health Clinic because of the ulcer and allergies which are thought to be due to emotional difficulties."

A hearing on the case by the juvenile court was scheduled for May 1, 1961, then postponed to September 1 (by that time Stella was in the psychiatric ward of the hospital, soon to be turned over to the jurisdiction of Montgomery County at that county's request).

The summer of 1961 and the Batson Road "rape" seemed to be one of rising frenzy for Stella in spite of the threat of probation.

"I think she is just one of those type of girls," Tom Brooks had written Harold, "that after she got a feel of sex she wanted a lot of it."

So it seemed to be. That was the summer, according to the affidavits of the boys who knew her, when "she liked to be the only girl to go out with a group of boys, and to have intercourse with the whole group"; when she "would get into cars with people she didn't know," and when, at a restaurant they all frequented, she would offer herself to any boy that would "pay her five dollars." The owner of a pizza shop told how she "usually came in to be picked up by boys, and when this happened, she would leave my place with them." These were also the days when—the boys said—she would perform a striptease act for groups, and would pose for pictures in the nude. "Stella liked to boast about her sex accomplishments," said another, adding, "I don't think she exaggerated."

"I have never known a girl that behaved anything like Stella Mae Watkins," said one affidavit. "She was forward about everything, particularly sex. For the few weeks that I knew her, she would have sexual relations with any boy any time he wanted to. On two occasions I saw her have sexual relations in an automobile with each of 3 or 4 boys. I had sexual relations with her two times, once in an automobile, and once in her house on Winterset Street, in the first bedroom on the right hand side of the door as you go into her house." (When Detective Wheeler of Prince George's police interviewed her in the hospital, in connection with the rape charge against the two white men, he reported her admission of "numerous acts of sexual intercourse and sodomy with many boys and men many of whom were unknown to her.")

On July 1, her parents went on a trip and Stella was supposed to stay with her married brothers, but she remained at home and the whole neighborhood was aware of the turmoil as boys came to the house at all hours of the day and night. On July 4, Stella herself reported them to the police because "they wanted her boyfriend to come out and fight." After her parents' return, the "carload of boys" continued coming, even though Mr. Watkins stood out in the yard, occasionally shooting off his gun from behind a bush, as one neighbor said. On July 20, of course, was the climactic episode on Batson Road, and about a month later the suicide attempt, the days in the psychiatric ward, and the rape charge against Glen Wykoff—"she stated that she had had sexual intercourse with the subject . . . on several occasions and had been perfectly willing in doing so." Whether she had previously had relations with Arthur Jones, also at the party, Detective Wheeler's report does not state. She had offered no resistance to either. "When questioned," his report continued, "as to why she offered no resistance she stated that she would have voluntarily had intercourse with both of these subjects but she thought if she did so at this location they would tell the other boys at the party and all would want to do this."

A psychiatrist also saw her in the hospital, diagnosing her as a case of "juvenile schizophrenia," although his diagnosis was not permitted in the court as evidence.

When Stella went to the hospital, her mother called Lieutenant Whalen of the Montgomery County police; she had talked to him before, in connection with the Giles-Johnson case, and she did so again now. How much of the situation he told Leonard Kardy, Prosecuting Attorney for the county, is not known. What is known is that Stella was brought before the juvenile court of that neighboring county, which decided to commit her to the Montrose School for girls, as "out of parental control and living in circumstances to endanger her well-being"; and also because said child is "a necessary witness in behalf of the State in regard to a criminal case pending in the Circuit Court."

The probation officer of this county filled in more of the background. The county reports about Stella reflected a family history of constant recrimination and disagreement. Stella herself said her home was partly responsible for her problem, because her father was so much older than her mother, and "a lot of it stems out of his jealousy and talk of sex, etc." It was "one brewing mess, all the time. He feels his job is to provide and that is all. It goes on and on until he tears things up, and then he replaces them."

Stella impressed people variously. The owner of a restaurant where she often sang folksongs on the weekends said, "She had a great personality, was old for her age, and knew how to handle people." In her neighborhood and at her high school she had her partisans.

The wife of a psychiatrist, Mrs. Prentiss, telephoned Harold at one point to say she was interested in the girl in the case, from what she had read, and could Harold tell her how to find out more about her. Being eager to find out more about her himself, Harold replied with the usual four-page, single-spaced letter and enclosures. He listed various names of those who could tell her about Stella, including two women "who, I heard, are hopping mad at me and at the committee. They might, therefore, be excellent people from whom to obtain an understanding of many things about which we are still in the dark."

Mrs. Prentiss elected to interview those two, and in turn reported the results to Harold. An administrator at the high school was angry. "I wouldn't *speak* to anyone on that committee. They sent someone out here; he painted a terribly black picture, so we opened up the records and we didn't find one thing. Then a reporter and his wife came out here and I looked at that woman and said, 'There but for the grace of God. You're going to have a baby. What if it should be a girl and this should happen to her?' I wouldn't tell them one thing. They should be ashamed of themselves. That girl was so hounded. She'd be getting along all right and then there'd be another story on the radio and she'd come in here crying. She just couldn't stand it. Why, one of our civics teachers talked about it in class. He said, 'What do you suppose would have happened if the boys had been white?' Then he said, 'And I hear the girl's reputation wasn't so good, either.' Stella came running down here after that class saying, 'I can't even go back to class.' I called that teacher in and said, 'Don't you *ever* make statements like that again, and furthermore, the girl who was involved was in your class.'

"Let's face it: none of us are perfect. So what if she wasn't lily-white? Did they have to spread it from one end of town to the other? Why, prostitutes have to be protected: you can't go out and rape someone just because she's had intercourse before."

A neighbor, Mrs. Prentiss reported, was "puzzled about the goals of the committee and extremely vengeful toward them . . . at one point she asked 'What does this Harold Knapp do? I wonder if he couldn't be stopped from that angle. He works in the Pentagon, I believe. We're spending our money to pay him and he spends all his time . . . doing this kind of thing to ruin a girl's life . . . . I just wonder what those people want to *do* to that family, just what do they want the poor girl to say? That it never happened? Do you have a daughter? What if this happened to her? Look at D.C. I suppose they're going to say that this new rape case is the same, that the men should be let off?"

"I understand," said Mrs. Prentiss, "she told the investigating officer in the hospital that she had been quite promiscuous."

"Oh, I would just love to have heard Stella telling that story," the neighbor answered. "I can just hear her. She loved to make up stories. That's just like her. If her mother accused her of something, she would just go ahead and exaggerate what she'd done. She'd never deny it. Now you go back and ask that committee if they haven't ever felt sorry for anyone."

At astonishingly frequent intervals during the years the committee was fighting to get at the truth of the case, someone would telephone Harold or Mrs. Ross with additional or new evidence. Sometimes the callers were motivated by conscience, sometimes by the nagging awareness that they were privy to special information.

One of these calls came from Robert Bruce, and was followed by an affidavit and a long letter telling his recollections of Stella, whom he had known some years before. He wrote from a Midwestern university where he was a graduate student. "I am trying to act like Marcel Proust," he wrote, "and failing miserably." On that last point, the committee disagreed.

Bruce reported that Stella had often sung with a band in which he played from 1960 to 1962, which became

> a most important segment of Stella's high school life. The band served as a springboard to a substantial part of her social life. It got her to fraternity parties, private beer clubs, Moose club dances and cheap nightclubs. We never knew what she would do at these functions . . . . One curious and important fact is that her relationships with members of the band were unlike her relationship with any other person or group. We were acquainted with her professionally (though I often wondered just what *was* her profession—singing or picking up lovers). Sometimes we acted as scolding fathers; sometimes we were merely an appreciative audience to her phenomenal talents of man-hunting. But we were never the object of her pursuit. Because of this I feel I can safely say that the band members are the only people who can talk about her with the utmost objectivity . . . . Because we were unfamiliar with the ways of Stella and her boys, we delighted in experiencing it vicariously—goading her into talking about her prowess.

Both Bruce and another band member remembered a conversation with Stella on the way home from an engagement.

> It began jokingly and then we unwittingly provoked her into reciting an imposing list of male associates with whom she had had sexual relations. I then said to her "Stella, if you don't change your ways you're going to get yourself raped someday," to which she replied, "If that situation ever came up, I'd just let it happen. I wouldn't resist." I am unable to quote the rest of the conversation, but she pointed out that after all, the act was the same, only the circumstances were different.
>
> When we first read about the alleged rape [on Batson Road] I called Don up and discovered we had each independently thought of the incident and remembered what she had said, exactly. Of course we hooted and howled and guffawed. It really was a ludicrous idea—Stella raped!

He had seen Stella shortly after the "rape."

I remember noticing her subdued manner. It struck me that she was really taking advantage of her sensational situation—playing the role of the wronged maiden. I thought, She really is playing this scene to the hilt! It was a stupid little act, specially considering that this was Stella who was trying to pull it off.

The frightening thing is that she has apparently pulled it off, in court. Has she?

XIII

Spring of 1964 . . . and where were they? Exactly nowhere, some of the committee members and surely the prisoners were thinking. For two and a half years every legal attempt had failed, and though they had succeeded in keeping Joe and the Giles alive, that was all that could be said on the credit side. What was the good of amassing more and more evidence to show that the boys were technically innocent of rape if there was no legal way to get a new trial to prove it?

At this stage, Joe Forer took charge of the defense because Hal Witt had given up private practice for a full-time government job. Thereafter, he helped on occasion and always assisted in the courtroom, but the major responsibility was Forer's. Twice Hal's age, he had argued before both juries and judges, including some twenty-five cases before the Justices of the Supreme Court. He was skilled and sardonic—"our disadvantage," he told the committee, "is that we have justice on our side"—with a strong distaste for sentimentality. He found it difficult to make an emotional appeal. Wit was another matter, and flashes of it often enlivened the courtroom, provided that the judge or judges appeared receptive to it.

He decided to request a "post-conviction hearing," a courtroom procedure which few on the committee had ever heard of and the logic of which seemed to them almost indefensible, having nothing to do with arriving at justice.

Suppose that a convicted man, only after his conviction has been affirmed on appeal, discovers new evidence that satisfies the court that at his trial a major prosecution witness gave important perjured testimony that might explain why the jury found him guilty. Will the convict obtain a new trial by what is called a "post-conviction remedy"?

Almost all our courts say "Only if the prosecutor knew during the trial that the witnesses lied; if so the conviction was unconstitutionally obtained. But if, at the time of the trial, the prosecution was ignorant of the deliberate falsity of the testimony, the conviction must stand."

This distinction derives from the theory that a criminal trial is a sort of prize fight. According to that theory, if the prosecutor knowingly introduced perjured testimony, he dealt the accused a foul blow and the government must surrender its "victory." But if the prosecutor used that testimony in good faith, then he did not fight unfairly and the government has a right to retain its "victory" over the accused.*

Whether the Giles and Joe Johnson had raped Stella Mae, or whether she had consented to intercourse had nothing to do with the case—the truth, in short, seemed not to matter.

"As Your Honor knows," said Forer, later in the courtroom, "it is the law for reasons which are no doubt obscure to many laymen and even to some lawyers—including myself—that in a post-conviction procedure the question of guilt or innocence is not relevant. The question is not even material, all by itself, whether the conviction was procured by perjured testimony. That is only an element. It is necessary to show that the State was at fault—the shorthand generally used among lawyers is that it must be shown that the State either knew of the perjury or induced it, or the State suppressed evidence."

The State was guilty, he went on to say, even if the prosecutor himself did not know that any evidence was being withheld, but an agent of the State—such as the police—had some evidence and was not revealing it.

* Jerome and Barbara Frank, *Not Guilty*, Doubleday, 1957.

To try to prove that the State of Maryland had been negligent in its conduct of the Giles-Johnson cases was not going to be easy. A post-conviction hearing would be a threat not only to Leonard Kardy, the prosecutor, but also to Lieutenant Whelan, who had conducted the police investigation, and to the two other policemen involved.

The fight began early in May and occupied most of it.

On May 11, Forer filed a petition with the Montgomery County Circuit Court seeking relief under the Post-Conviction Procedure Act, requesting that the conviction of the Giles brothers be set aside and that they either be released from prison or granted a new trial on the grounds that their convictions had been "procured by testimony which was perjured, which the State knew was perjured, and some of which perjured testimony the State induced . . . [and that] the State suppressed and withheld material exculpatory evidence and thereby was enabled to, and did, give at the trial a false and misleading impression of the facts."

On May 18, he served notice of the "Taking of Depositions" for the purpose of "exploring the knowledge of certain witnesses and some official records." (Depositions taken in a courtroom before a judge are far more legally binding than affidavits, which are only notarized. False statements in a deposition could subject one to perjury charges.)

On May 19, the State filed an "Answer" denying the allegations of Forer's petition requesting a post-conviction hearing.

On May 20, the State asked the Court to dismiss the notice of the "Taking of Depositions."

On May 22, Judge Walter Moorman heard arguments from both sides.

On May 26, he refused to dismiss the notice (of deposition taking).

On May 27, Kardy asked the Court of Appeals to reverse Moorman, saying depositions were properly taken only in civil, not criminal, cases. "We have nothing to hide," he said, "and if the Court of Appeals rules for the defense, we will be delighted to cooperate in any way."

On May 28—for the first time in the history of the Giles-Johnson case—the Appeals Court *did* rule for the defense, approving both the taking of depositions and the subsequent post-conviction hearing.

On May 29, in a final gesture of recalcitrance, Lieutenant Whelan, who had been called to give the first deposition, refused to speak on orders from Leonard Kardy, because the Giles brothers were not present. Since their presence was not legally required, and only the State could extract them from prison in any event, the Court ordered Whelan to appear.

On June 22, the depositions were at last taken.

"Trying to understand the maneuvering which has been going on in the Giles-Johnson case post-conviction proceedings," wrote Les Kimble in the Montgomery County *Sentinel,* "is for the observer like watching some strange game for the first time. . . . If the allegations of the defense attorneys are mistaken, then one would think that the State would be eager to have additional testimony and hearings in the record. Assuming the State is correct, one is left with the conclusion that the legal maneuvering by the State serves some obscure legal purpose or serves to prolong the contest. The public is now more interested in the truth than the contest. Public interest will continue to grow until this case is fully and completely explored."

The performance on that June day proved much like a dress rehearsal for the post-conviction hearing a month later. The same Judge Moorman presided at both. He had been a lawyer with the Navy for twenty-five years, retired to Montgomery County, and served it as a trial magistrate until he was elected judge in 1962. He was in his late fifties, with crinkly gray hair and bushy gray eyebrows from beneath which he peered at each witness coming into the box with an intent, studying stare, before he turned back to face the attorneys. Some in the cast of characters would appear again: a psychiatrist and a physician, Lieutenant Whelan and Mrs. Watkins. Stella Mae's deposition was taken, but in the end—though waiting—she was not called at the hearing.

Judge Moorman's courtroom manner was genial, but once he had taken a position, nothing could persuade him to change it.

"Gentlemen," he said at the start, "I would like to state at the outset that . . . the taking of this testimony is going to be limited to the suppression of evidence and to perjury as alleged with the knowledge of the State's Attorney. It is limited to that."

And limit it he did, as he sustained objection after objection. He refused to let either doctor say anything about Stella Mae's mental health; he refused to let into evidence the rape charge she made and subsequently withdrew against the two white men; he refused any report of the juvenile court hearing, evidence vital to the defense because Whelan—"agent of the state"—had been at that hearing. Had he "withheld material exculpatory evidence" at the trial when he made no mention of Stella's having been brought before that court?

Mrs. Watkins's answers to Forer's questions consisted mainly of "I don't recall," and her daughter also proved unable to remember. She couldn't remember having said at the first hearing that only two men had raped her, but she could remember positively that she had told the police "three."

Forer had a strong suspicion that the original police reports and interviews might be of crucial importance, and might show both William Rogers and Stella Mae to have been lying on the witness stand. At the trial in 1961, Stedman Prescott testified that Kardy had shown him "his entire file" on the case. But Forer wanted to be sure. He pleaded with Moorman:

How do you prove it is to the knowledge of the State's Attorney? You start by finding out that the police knew it, and then did the police tell the State's Attorney. That is why we are entitled to the interview report, Your Honor.

. . . . .

The Court: I will not permit the police report to be produced, because as I understand the law under the Rules of Civil Procedure it is a work product.

In the course of deposing Lieutenant Whelan, Forer tried again:

Q. But would your interview report of this interview show what Stella Watkins said about the number of men who attacked her?
A. Yes, sir.
Forer: Your Honor, we ask that the witness be instructed to produce for our inspection the police report of the interview with Stella Watkins.
Kardy: I object.
The Court: The objection will be sustained, for the reasons that I gave before, Mr. Forer.
Forer: Your Honor, this is the bind we are in. On the one hand . . . .

Earlier, the judge had commented:

The Court: This is the bind the Court is in, too. We are a government of laws, and regardless of what I think—if I could make the law, Mr. Forer, I would order the State's Attorney in every criminal case to give them the whole record, give them all the police reports—but I do not make the law, and maybe it is a good thing I do not. . . .

On the whole it was a discouraging day.

While the legal maneuvering and infighting was going on, the committee was busy trying to contribute what it could. The members got out a press release on their reaction to Kardy's efforts to block the deposition taking. They sent out a letter to their long list of potential contributors asking for funds, and

131

they staged a party in the garden of one of their sponsors (who now numbered sixty-five and made an impressive list on their letter-head paper) to raise money. They needed money: each deposition cost fifty dollars, and preparing petitions and appeals and replies to appeals took money. Joe Forer should have been receiving money but, like Hal Witt, he charged nothing. Nevertheless, the committee wanted to pay him any extra it could scrape up.

Harold Knapp continued to pursue William Rogers. He managed to catch up with him for two evenings, and though he gave him a lot to drink and employed all his persuasiveness, William remained wary and the affidavit Harold had prepared remained unsigned.

He was still pursuing other people as well. On June 29 he wrote to Dotty Brooks: "Only 10 affidavits to go, now, plus a press release, plus a complete report on the case before the Hearing . . . Reached 150 pounds today. [This was the time he began running four miles each day when he got home from work, a habit he continued.] From 206. That does it. Ah is now slim, trim and GRIM! We've been getting phone calls all night long."

(These phone calls consisted sometimes of a few insults or obscenities hurled across the line, and sometimes of no words at all, but only the sound of breathing at the other end. The Knapps kept a record of the time and content of each call.)

Through the mail one day came the following:

Declaration

John Watkins, Plaintiff, vs. Harold A. Knapp, Defendant.

John Watkins is a Police Officer on the Metropolitan Police Department of the District of Columbia, who resides in Prince George's County, Maryland.

Harold A. Knapp's capacity is unknown, but he resides in Montgomery County, Maryland.

On, or about, June 12, 1963, Harold A. Knapp with malice aforethought in the District of Columbia did tell . . . the immediate superior of the Plaintiff, certain things that were untrue and slanderous, per se . . . did willfully and maliciously state that said John Watkins had taken advantage of his position as a police officer when dealing with the Defendant on a personal matter . . . to detriment of Plaintiff . . . .

WHEREFORE Plaintiff demands $25,000 in compensatory damages and $150,000 in punitive damages . . . Plaintiff demands trial by jury on all issues herein.

> by Walter Biernbaum
> Attorney for Plaintiff

At first glance Harold thought the declaration some kind of mistake. Then he remembered the episode a year before when he had been dragged down the steps of Stella's house, had been threatened and almost run over by John Watkins at the gas station, and subsequently had called the D.C. police to report the conduct of their man. He talked to Joe Forer about the declaration and dismissed it from his mind.

He was reminded of it a few nights later when the phone rang at almost two in the morning. The call was from the lawyer who had written the declaration. He signaled Barbara to get on the other phone. She came on in time to hear Harold ask: "Are you calling me psychotic?"

"Yes, and you are an unmitigated liar."

"Have you anything else to tell me, Mr. Biernbaum?"

"The rest I will tell you in the courtroom, when we take your money from you."

"Good night," said Harold, and hung up.

Again he dismissed the declaration, because he had no time to think of anything except his work and finishing the Blue Report.

The Blue Report—so called because of its blue covers— hung over the heads of the Knapps and of the other committee members with a compelling urgency. ("The man who gets it all on paper wins," Harold repeated.) They wanted that report to be as definitive as they could make it. Some of it—those parts which had been adequately covered in the report to the Governor a year before—could be reproduced now, and were. But Harold wanted much more to go into this: all the new affidavits, new letters, and a section called "The Defense's Version of Events." He wanted everything covered right up to the forthcoming post-conviction hearing on July 20, and as those nervous, pressured days got closer to the deadline, he became increasingly a perfectionist, and a taskmaster. "It doesn't matter whether it costs money, or time. It's got to be done."

During the last ten days, committee members marketed for Barbara, and prepared meals while she attempted to write some remaining sections, type others, edit what Harold wrote, and keep the whole in order. The Knapps' big playroom in the basement became headquarters, and there several people worked on sorting and assembling. To the extent there were beds, they slept at the Knapps', as well as ate there. The Alts' daughter Theresa helped Barbara with the typing and would work as long as she could physically stand it, then fall into bed, wake herself about four, and start on it again. They hoped to have the report—every bit of which had to be checked by Joe Forer for libel—ready and distributed to the press and radio a week before the hearing, but by Saturday, nine days before the deadline, they had not begun to be finished.

On that same Saturday, Gunnar Knapp was to spend the night at Dotty Brooks's. Late in the evening, with Jim Alt and Emily in the car, Harold drove Gunnar to Dotty's. On the way home, they drove down the street on which Stella's house was at the end. Harold stopped for the stop sign and—yielding to impulse—beeped the horn of the Volkswagen once. In a flash, Mrs. Watkins was off her front porch with a bottle in her hand which she brought down full force on the rear of the car. Furious, Harold drove to the nearest police station, told the story, exhibited the dent in the car, and went back home to make another attempt to write certain remaining sections of the Blue Report.

There was, those days, very little "singing with papa."

By noon on Thursday of the following week, Barbara saw that they could not possibly get the material to the mimeographers the next day. Would the place work on Saturday? It would, though of course the men would have to be paid overtime.

Friday night proved to be the last of bedlam. The arguments over what should go into the report had, of necessity, come to an end, but Harold had yet to finish some writing and "The Defense's Version of Events" had still to be done.

"Jane Thayer took time off from her research to come out that night," said Barbara, "and Harold got one of the secretaries from the Pentagon who was interested in the case to come out. She was a professional and could type lots faster than I could. That left me free to edit. But here was Harold, still not approving anything he wrote and we still had to guess at the number of pages because what he had to write was to go in the middle. And here was the secretary trying to type and complaining about my typewriter. Then Harold fell asleep on the couch because he just couldn't think anymore and I was still trying frantically to put down on paper a Defense's Version that wouldn't be libelous. Then Jane Thayer had an inspiration: that we could do it entirely through excerpts from the trial transcript, with dashes for omissions. That way we'd be safe on libel.

"Somehow that suggestion made everything click. We got it down on paper pretty fast; Harold woke up and managed at last to get the other parts done; the secretary was going right on complaining, but we all felt better. I suppose we got to bed about three or four—we hardly slept at all during those weeks —and the next day we took the secretary along to the mimeographing place and she used their electric typewriter.

"Everybody turned up there. The place was in Washington, near the Mayflower. There was a crew of the nicest men, all Negroes, who were so much interested in what we were doing. The rest of us did the assembling as the pages came off the machines. It was late Saturday night before we finished up.

"Then we had to hand-carry the copies: that was when I compiled that list of the home addresses of all the press reporters and the radio and TV ones. The Alts and Frances Ross and we took on various routes and we delivered Saturday night and Sunday. It wasn't what we'd hoped for—we'd wanted them to have a whole week to study it—but we got a lot of press coverage anyway."

"The two Giles brothers and Joseph Johnson," said a *Washington Post* editorial (October 31, 1963), titled "Justice on Trial," "would be dead today but for the efforts of several private citizens. Had the Giles's mother not been employed by Mrs. Howard Ross, there would have been no Giles-Johnson Defense Committee. Had Harold Knapp not written a letter about the case to a weekly newspaper, and had John Giles not answered it from prison, Mr. Knapp would not have embarked upon the months of patient detective work that won the three young men's commutation. On this fragile concatenation of coincidence hung three men's lives . . . ."

XIV

"Are the petitioners ready?" asked Judge Moorman.

"Petitioners are ready," answered Joe Forer.

"Is the State ready?" asked Judge Moorman.

"The State is ready," answered Leonard Kardy.

The people in circuit courtroom #1 were also ready on July 20, 1964. The Knapps had been there for almost an hour, sitting in the front row to the right. On the seat beside them was a large box of Blue Reports which the sheriff had given Harold permission to sell to any interested spectator. The piles of 230 legal-size bound pages sold with surprising speed at two dollars a report, bringing in money that would help defray the expense of having had it mimeographed.

By 9:30, the court was full and people were standing at the rear. The box usually occupied by a jury was also full, this time with members of the press. John and James Giles, in dark, penitentiary-produced suits, sat in the front row in the center of the room, flanked by guards; and beyond the walnut partition were Joe Forer and Hal Witt at one table and Leonard Kardy and his assistant Cromwell at another. Black-robed Judge Moorman was in his high leather chair.

Joe Forer led off with his opening statement, summarizing quickly the events of that night on Batson Road—three years before to the day—and, after mentioning the Governor's com-

mutation, came closer to the key issues which the hearing was
to resolve.

> As Your Honor can see, it went to the jury as a question of
> credibility. The question was: would the jury believe the
> story that the Giles brothers told, that the altercation at the
> car had been provoked by William Rogers's profanity and that
> the girl had solicited intercourse? Or would they believe the
> story of William Rogers and Stella Watkins, that the alterca-
> tion had been provoked by the Giles brothers' demanding the
> girl, and that the girl had not solicited intercourse but had
> merely submitted out of fear . . . there were certain weak-
> nesses, let us say, in connection with the credibility of those
> witnesses . . . . But there were even greater weaknesses, as far
> as a jury could judge, in the story of the defendants. They
> would have to believe that this sixteen-year-old girl, sixteen-
> year-old white girl in the dark woods with three young
> Negroes around her, if she did what they said she did, she
> must have been incredibly wanton. And in order to believe
> their version, that William Rogers did what they said he did
> . . . he provokes an altercation by calling them vile names,
> he had to be an incredibly reckless boy, and I suppose it is
> no wonder that the jury believed the story of the prosecu-
> tion . . . . We intend to show that William Rogers's and Stella
> Watkins' story was false, and that of the Giles brothers
> [true]."

He mentioned then the question of guilt or innocence, of
who was telling the truth and who lying.

> "[The three boys] had never seen this girl before in their lives
> . . . she certainly could have said she was in trouble because
> she was. There was no other way that John and James Giles
> could have known that she was in this status of on or close to
> probation or in trouble unless, in fact, she did tell them she
> was on probation and would have to call rape, and if she did
> tell them some of the other things it wasn't rape. Because no
> girl in the middle of being raped, or in anticipation of being
> raped, tells her attackers such things [as] "I've had sixteen
> or seventeen other boys earlier this week . . ."

That was a curious statement for the defendants to have made up, he said, and indeed they had not.

> [We have evidence that] that was the line she used when talking with young men with whom she was having or about to have, intercourse . . . and we have evidence that she was incredibly promiscuous with other men to the point where it can well be said she was suffering from nymphomania, and by definition, rape, being intercourse against the will of a woman . . . it is virtually impossible to rape a nymphomania[c].

Next he swung back to the basic requirement for the defense, that of proving "the involvement of the State in connection with this miscarriage of justice," and that the State was "guilty of one of several types of reprehensible conduct." The word "suppression" was misleading, he said, "because you no longer have to show suppression in the sense that the State destroyed some evidence or secreted a witness." He cited cases.

> This law that I have been describing has been carried even further by a modern trend of what might almost be called negligent suppression, and that there are certain instances where even if the State does not know the facts which have been withheld, if the State was very much at fault in not knowing these facts, it is going to be charged with knowledge.
>
> The theory being that the State is not entitled, when a man's life or liberty is at stake, and when it has indications there may be something wrong with its case, it is not entitled to close its eyes and refuse to look further. And that is the type of involvement we expect to show here . . . . Let me go on to specifics.

These came down to the claims that (1) William Rogers had been told to lie and deny he had cursed the Negroes; (2) a policeman gave false testimony, saying that Stella had not told him before the trial that only two men had had intercourse with her; (3) Lieutenant Whelan knew Stella was mentally disturbed; (4) the authorities in Montgomery County knew

Stella was in a near-probation status—"if they didn't know it
. . . it was . . . because they willfully closed their eyes to information that was in the hands of police officers"; and (5) the
State knew the girl was promiscuous even though it did not
know the extent of the promiscuity "as we now know . . . [that]
was because the State showed gross carelessness, gross reckless-
ness in failing to follow up leads which they had, information
in their possession which should have placed an obligation on
them before seeking . . . the death of three young men . . ."

Any attempt "to rectify this manifest miscarriage of mis-
justice [was prevented] by what I can only describe as an ante-
diluvian rule"—the Three-Day Rule—"so extreme that in itself
it is an unconstitutional requirement. I know Your Honor
doesn't agree with me."

Judge Moorman broke in: "How do you know I don't?"

"Very well, Your Honor. I take it back. I hope you do."

And then he concluded with an apology for having taken so
long, "but there is a great deal at stake here. Thank you very
much."

He returned to his chair at the counsels' table and poured
himself a glass of water. Hal Witt gave him a quick smile of
approval. John, always with the shadow of sadness on his face,
sat impassive, brooding; James showed no hint of feeling, but
his eyelids kept blinking with the nervous tic that had begun
in this same courtroom.

Leonard Kardy rose now to make his far briefer opening
statement, his blue-green silk suit flashing in the light, his blue
and white shoes freshly polished. He had been in the State's
Attorney's office for ten years, he said, during which he had
never asked for the death penalty, and he never would. It was
the jury's job to convict or not. As to Stella's juvenile record,

> The Court ruled as a matter of law that juvenile records are
> inadmissible . . . and in the rape case the fact to be deter-
> mined by the Court and by a jury if it is being tried before a

jury . . . and prior acts of intercourse are inadmissible unless
with the same defendant. That is a rule of cardinal, ele-
mental, fundamental law in these United States and juvenile
records are not admissible . . . that is why the jury never
heard that evidence . . . so the sole issue here is whether the
State, myself as State's Attorney, knowingly used perjured
testimony, induced State witnesses to perjure themselves and
that . . . I suppressed evidence . . . . We say to you with all
candor and as an officer of this court and State's Attorney for
this county, that that was not done. Thank you, Your Honor."
The Court: Call your witness.
Forer: Call Thomas John Brooks.

So here was Tom again coming in through the door at the
back of the witness box, looking young, scared, and vulnerable.
When he had testified before, at Joe Johnson's trial in Annapolis, only a few people were there. Today, the big courtroom had no empty seats and spectators stood three deep at
the back. Though he was now in the service at Fort Monmouth,
he wore civilian clothes. Scared or not, he did not swerve from
his story, even on cross-examination by Kardy. He had known
William Rogers for fifteen years, and Stella maybe for five.
After William had testified at Joe Johnson's trial, Tom had
driven him home and asked how things had gone in court that
day. "Pretty good," Rogers had said; he'd just done what he
was told to by the "lawyers, the men that brought him there . . .
State lawyers." He had been asked to play up Stella as a nice
girl and not to say he had cursed at the Negroes.

> Forer: I want to leave that and go back to an earlier matter,
>   the episode in 1961. Did you hear about that episode right
>   after it happened?
> A.   Yes.
> Q.   All right . . . when was the last time you saw Stella
>   Watkins before that Thursday?
> A.   Saturday before that Thursday.
> Q.   Was it in the daytime or the nighttime?

A.   Night.

Q.   Where did you meet her?

A.   At a place called California Inn, in Laurel, Maryland.

Q.   Did you meet her there by pre-arrangement?

A.   No, accidental . . . .

Q.   Now did you and she leave the California Inn and go Somewhere?

A.   Yes.

Q.   Did you have a discussion with her as to where you would go?

A.   Yes . . . she said she did not want to go down into the Hyattsville, Maryland area because she was in trouble on her probation.

Q.   Now, where did you go?

A.   We stayed at Laurel and went preferably to my house.

Q.   And what did you do at your house?

A.   Went swimming and had sexual relations . . . .

Q.   Now tell us the conversation . . . .

Kardy: Your Honor, I object. This is before the crime.

The Court: I think it is important, Mr. Kardy. I will hear it.

A.   Oh, I said, "Well, how can you like me so very much with the fact that you had so many relationships with other boys?" She says, she says, that just the last week-end in Baltimore that she went to a party, she was the only girl and there were about sixteen boys there and she had relations with all of them.

Kardy: Object.

Forer: Your Honor, we are not introducing this as evidence of chastity or unchastity . . . but as proof that Stella had a line. The line was to brag that she had sixteen or seventeen other boys a few nights before . . . .

The Court: I am going to sustain the objection and move it out of the record.

Forer: Are you familiar with Stella's reputation for chastity?

A.   Yes.

Q.   What is that reputation?

Kardy [throwing his pencil on table in disgust]:   Object.

Forer: May I speak to the relevance? My main point is to show the girl was promiscuous to an extraordinary extent. However, I shall stop talking on this point and refer Your

142

Honor to the affidavit of Thomas John Brooks, specifically paragraphs 4, 5, and 6.

Judge Moorman read them, looked up, and said, "Objection sustained." Tom Brooks endured Kardy's cross-examination and gratefully left the box.

In an editorial printed before this hearing, the *Washington Post* (May 18, 1964) had said:

> The issue now reaches far beyond the three men in prison. Of all the new evidence that the Defense Committee has put forward, the most telling is taken from the Police and Juvenile Court Records of Prince George's County. It is a staggering indictment to say that the prosecution asked for three men's lives without knowing all that this little band of amateurs has published. The Giles's lawyers charge, of course, that the prosecution did know, and that conclusion is even more staggering. In a strange reversal of roles, the prosecution must now defend itself.

What was in those Prince George's County records, and in those of the juvenile court of Montgomery County was crucial, as both sides knew. They had already been in evidence before the Governor. Today, Forer was armed with written authorization from the courts to introduce them, in accordance with Maryland's Rule 922 of the Annotated Code. But Judge Moorman ruled against their being admitted. Forer pleaded:

> The language of the statute . . . is not to protect the juvenile at all costs, in a case like this where somebody else's liberty depends on finding out certain facts as to the juvenile . . . . We are not introducing these facts per se, as Your Honor knows. Whether these facts are true or not is irrelevant. As the Court knows, this is very striking . . . that this knowledge [derived from the two juvenile court records] "was in the possession of Montgomery County officials at the time the petitioners were tried."

This was evidence that the State suppressed knowledge of the fact respecting her credibility at the trial because, he went on to point out, Lieutenant Whelan, an agent of the State, had not only set up that juvenile court hearing in Montgomery County in the first place, but had attended the hearing.

It was no use. Back went all those records for refiling in the two counties.

The onlookers were puzzled. The committee members were inclined to like Judge Moorman. It was hard not to. He seemed an altogether human judge and they found appealing the gesture he used when trying to decide whether or not to sustain an objection: he would make a broad swipe across his face, with his opened right hand, bring it to rest before mouth and chin, then lower it and deliver his decision, all too frequently against the defendants.

After Tom, a Doctor Connor was called as witness. He had seen Stella Mae daily in the hospital after her suicide attempt, and had discussed her case with "someone from Montgomery County Police Department." He couldn't remember the name. That was as much as the Court would let him discuss, nor was it willing to admit the conclusions of a psychiatrist ("juvenile schizophrenia") at the deposition taking. An official of the juvenile court of Montgomery County testified that Lieutenant Whelan had been present at its hearing on the subject of Stella Mae. Had it been brought out at that hearing, the defense asked, that Stella had tried to commit suicide, and that she had accused two white men of raping her? Moorman permitted no answers and, indeed, seemed to think that any information concerning a juvenile was sacrosanct. The committee and the lawyers could only hope he would read the affidavits.

In the afternoon Elston Finch appeared in the box, one of the group from whom Dotty Brooks and Harold had coaxed an affidavit that blizzardy morning back in the winter. He was slim, white-faced, with a concave profile, and his moving jaws revealed the gum which from time to time he tried to hide in his cheek. He had seen Stella a couple of nights after the Batson Road incident, and she had said "something to me about she had been raped and they were bigger and better [than white boys]." Kardy objected, but Moorman let it remain in evidence, although he permitted Elston to say nothing further. Neither was Evelyn Clark allowed to say in the courtroom what she had said in her affidavit. So Hal Witt "proferred" that if she had testified she would have said William Rogers was "an extremely bellicose individual; that he would start fights on numerous occasions without provocation . . . even if he was outnumbered; that he was a notorious barroom brawler . . . and that he also habitually used [the racial epithet that the Giles and Joe Johnson claimed he had]." Jacqueline Giles testified that Harding, one of the policemen who had come to their house the morning of July 21, 1961, had quoted Stella as saying only two of the boys had raped her. And the affidavit of Mrs. Giles to the same effect was admitted as testimony, since she was no longer living.

Next came Mark White, who had driven Stella and William to the Rock that night and left them in his car while he went to get gas. He sat unintimidated in the box, in a green T-shirt, sideburns framing his face. Had he, Forer asked, had a bathing suit with him?

> The Court: I can't see what that has to do with rape.
> Forer: The State knew there was no bathing suit in the car. That was a piece of false testimony given by William Rogers which was false and the State knew was false.
> The Court: Objection overruled.
> White: I didn't have a bathing suit, no.

Detective Wheeler of Prince George's County had interviewed Stella in the hospital, but admitted, to Kardy's questions, that no official from Montgomery County (Kardy's) had ever come to ask him what he had found out in that interview.

The matter of the two neighboring counties came up again when Forer vainly attempted to pin down Lieutenant Whelan on certain points, as he had tried when taking his deposition. Whelan had heard about "Stella's taking some pills," and the "unfounded rape charge," and he knew her mother had taken her to a psychiatrist. Yes, he had arranged the juvenile court hearing on Stella's case, but he had been "in and out of the room" while it went on. Why had he arranged that hearing in the first place?

> Whelan: I received a call from Mrs. Watkins, the girl's mother, that the boys in the area were harassing the girl so bad that she would like to get some help for the girl. I contacted Mr. Kardy, and the girl was brought before Juvenile Court.
>
> . . . . .
>
> Forer: Didn't you raise with Mrs. Watkins or with Mr. Kardy the question of Stella—that there was some question as to the jurisdiction in the Montgomery County Court because she was a resident of Prince George's County?
> Whelan: Not to my knowledge. No, sir.
>
> . . . . .
>
> Forer: Did you tell Judge Noyes [at that juvenile court hearing] that Stella Watkins was beyond parental control and a juvenile delinquent as well as a necessary witness for the State?
> Kardy: Object.
> Forer: These are the charges, Your Honor.
> The Court: I will overrule the objection.
> Whelan: I never gave him that information as to she was out of parental control . . . .
> Forer: Lieutenant Whelan, when you testified that you received a call that Stella Watkins had been raped in August in Prince George's County [the white men] you said that should be taken up with the Prince George's Police Department . . . .
> Whelan: That is correct, sir.

Forer: Then when you received a call, a later call, saying
that Stella was being bothered by some boys in Prince
George's County, then you went and arranged juvenile
court proceedings in Montgomery County?
Whelan: Correct, sir.

And at no time, Whelan said, had he made any pre-trial investigation of the characters or records of Stella, William, the
Giles, or Joe Johnson.

The Court recessed at 4:30, but the committee lingered in the
corridor, talking, speculating, far too stimulated to want to
leave. Harold, incorrigibly hospitable, kept saying to everyone,
"Come out to the house. Come for dinner." In the end, only a
few went, declined dinner, and soon left. Dotty Brooks took
Emily and Gunnar home with her for dinner and the night.

"You both look exhausted," she said to Barbara.

"We are. But Harold's promised that after he runs and eats
he'll go straight to bed, and I'm going to take the telephone off
the hook, so that nothing will wake us up."

Indeed they were exhausted. In addition to the sleeplessness
of the last few weeks and the strain of concentration in court,
there was the uneasiness created by another declaration. One
had been handed to Harold, another to Frances Ross, and a
third to Hal Witt as they had come into the court that morning.
They announced a suit brought by the Watkins family against
the three of them for $3,000,000. claiming "character defama-
tion, slander and invasion of privacy," in the course of the
hour-long radio program in the early fall of 1963, a year before.
None of the three on that program had mentioned Stella by
name, but the same Walter Biernbaum had contrived eleven
counts against them. Harold could say that he was flattered
by the implication that he had a million dollars. But it had not
been as easy to dismiss this suit from his mind as it had been
to dismiss the first declaration.

He kept his promise and was in bed before eight o'clock, but Barbara was still up when, a little after 10:00, she caught sight of an automobile on the county road below the ridge. Few cars went along there in the daytime, and almost none at night. To her dismay she watched it turn up their driveway, lighting the trees on either side. Before it had come to a stop in their carport, she had locked the front door and waked Harold. In the dark she fumbled to find clothes for him, and as they came out into the living room they could see that the car had turned off its lights and two figures—flashlights in hand—were approaching the door.

"Who is it?"

"Montgomery County police."

"Go around the house, to the right," said Harold, "so that I can see who you are."

He turned the floodlight on to that terrace beyond the dining room, where the family band practiced. There stood two uniformed police. He opened the door to them.

"Warrant for your arrest," they said, and read him part of it: "Case 9667 cr was charged by Citizen Catherine Watkins with 'acting in a disorderly manner to the disturbance of the public peace, making loud or unseemly noises at, upon, or near to 1603 Winterset Street . . . disturbing the peace, quiet, and order of said County contrary to the form of the Act of Assembly in such case made and provided and against the peace, government and dignity of the State.' "

It was sworn by and dated July 12, 1964.

"Why did you wait till July twentieth, after ten o'clock at night?" asked Harold, but he was given no answer other than that he must come with them to the Rockville police station for later transportation to the Prince George's station where he could arrange to post bond or pay collateral. He was given time to call Joe Forer, who said he had no alternative but to go; to get his briefcase, a toothbrush, and discover that between them

148

he and Barbara had not much more than five dollars in cash, and a check would be unacceptable. If Emily and Gunnar had been at home, Barbara could have set out to drive to neighbors to borrow money. But she could not leave Tina at home alone. They settled on the possibility that Dotty Brooks could borrow cash, if she did not have it on hand, and lived relatively close to the Prince George's station.

Barbara watched the lights of the police car go down the driveway. Then she sat down in a chair and laughed. "This is really too much," she said to Dotty when she got her on the telephone. "But at least they didn't get him last week before the Blue Report was finished!"

Yes, Dotty would raise the money: "Our neighbors will have some, even if Don and I don't have enough," and she would get to the police station, take Harold back to her house for the night, and have him to the courthouse the next morning.

"I made some other calls, too," said Barbara. "I thought the press ought to know. When I called the City Desk at the *Post,* I could hear the reporter turn to the others in the room and say, 'Get a load of this.' " She then went to bed, but in the end got little more sleep than did Harold.

Harold had occupied the trip to the Montgomery County station in Rockville with telling the two policemen the story of the night Mrs. Watkins had darted off her porch and banged a bottle on the rear of his Volkswagen, a fact he had providentially reported immediately to the Hyattsville Prince George's County police. At Rockville he was given a cup of coffee and a chance to call Barbara. He was then photographed and fingerprinted. He was handed police forms to fill out: his personal history, present and past employment, aliases, scars, nicknames, and the names of places he frequented. The forms, he was told, would be sent to the F.B.I., but if he were found not guilty, they could be withdrawn. And then—for it was 1:00 A.M. before a private from the Prince George's Police Force came

149

to drive him to the Hyattsville Station—he passed the time by telling the sergeant in charge the story of the Giles case. "I promised him I'd send him a copy of the Blue Report," said Harold in the ten-page documentary report he wrote on the whole episode, "and he seemed interested."

When he finally reached Hyattsville, he found Dotty waiting with the needed cash. He filled out still more forms, and at 3:00 in the morning he and Dotty finally reached the Brookses' house. In the courtroom the next morning, the night's events made a dramatic story.

XV

Tuesday, July 21, 1964, found John and James back in their seats in the front row; the lawyers at their tables; the press dilatory in arriving; far fewer people in the audience but most of the committee members back in the center seats at the front. On the dot of 9:30 the clerk pounded the gavel, the audience rose, the judge stomped in, all were seated, and the second day of the post-conviction hearing on Miscellaneous Petition No. 3005 began.

Stedman Prescott was first on the stand, to reveal, as he answered the Defense's questions, how he had been unable to get any information at all on which to base his defense, except the stories the Giles and Joe Johnson had told him. Kardy's cross-examination had to do exclusively with his, Kardy's, actions:

Q. Mr. Prescott, after your appointment . . . did you come to see me as State's Attorney for Montgomery County to discuss the case?

A. I did.

Q. And would you relate to his Honor what, if anything, I let you see and have on the case?

A. You let me have your entire file, as I recall . . . .

Q. And by the entire file, did I let you read the police report in its entirety, sir?

A. You did.

Detective Kennedy, who had examined the car on Batson Road, testified that he had found no bathing suits in it. Next, Hal Witt questioned Mrs. Watkins, who leaned forward slightly in the box, earrings swinging. She proved not unattractive as she parried Witt's questions. When she was angry, she threw back one shoulder and then the other; her hate seemed to spew out into the room. But when she seemed to be caught in a bit of testimony contrary to what she had said on her deposition, she would look first at Judge Moorman, then at Witt, an ingenuous smile would lift the corners of her mouth, and even the most adverse in the courtroom found it difficult to dislike her at those moments (except Harold Knapp, whose memory of his sleepless night in the police stations was still too vivid).

On the whole she made a tedious witness: she didn't know, she couldn't recall, she didn't remember. She was particularly obtuse about the meeting at the juvenile court of Montgomery County when Stella was committed to the Montrose School for Delinquent Girls. She hedged and paused, and started to speak and paused again, until even Kardy came in with, "If you know, Mrs. Watkins." More than once Judge Moorman tried to question her himself, and had to give up, saying to Hal Witt, "Ask her another question." The one point she reiterated was that everything had been peaceful in the Watkins household until the "rape" on Batson Road.

At last Hal Witt asked Moorman, "Your indulgence for a moment, Your Honor," had a quick conference with Joe Forer, and then said, "We have no further questions," adding that the defense was willing to excuse Miss Stella Watkins, who was waiting in the witness room. The State was also willing, and the session moved on to other witnesses and a repetition of "Objection. Sustained."

Midway through the morning, Joe Forer rose and said, "Your

Honor, the next witness we will call is an adverse witness. We call Mr. Kardy."

Kardy, conservatively dressed that day in a gray suit, went to the witness box and was sworn in. And then, to the relief of all, Judge Moorman said, "Let's take a ten-minute recess now and get our blood pressure down."

Blood pressure subsided somewhat over Cokes and cigarettes in the ten minutes, and though it rose again afterward, it was held to a gentlemanly, noblesse-oblige-between-lawyers level, even if, on occasion, Joe Forer's voice took on an edge of acrimony. Kardy sat easily in the witness chair and looked directly into Joe Forer's quizzical gray eyes out of his own round, flashing brown ones. Kardy had known nothing, nothing of Stella Mae's background; he had made no inquiries; he had shown Prescott his entire file though Maryland law did not require him to do so. He then embarked on a disquisition on Maryland law. Once launched, he continued until Moorman broke in:

> The Court: I think you had better ask him another question.
> Forer: I have been waiting for him to complete his answer.
> The Court: You are giving Mr. Kardy—he's not campaign-ing now, but you are really giving him a chance.
> Kardy: I am not campaigning, Your Honor.
> The Court: I think it's very good, Mr. Kardy, go right ahead.
> Forer: You'll have to convince me to vote for him.

At 1:00, the lunch recess was called and the Court was told to reconvene at 2:15. Lunch was a puzzled time for the committee members. It all appeared so clear to them: nobody seemed deliberately to have destroyed or hidden evidence, but —obsessed as they were with the determination to free the Giles and Joe Johnson of guilt—failure to investigate seemed quite as vital as a sin of commission.

153

On reconvening the Court, Moorman spoke with a stern face:

> "Counsel, Petitioners and the parties to this trial, and the spectators, it has been called to my attention during the recess that persons interested in this case have been selling, word hawking has been used, certain terminology to this case in the Courtroom, or the Courthouse steps and the corridors of the Courthouse. I am compelled to tell you that this type of thing is improper. Those of you who may be here, who have been doing that, must cease to do it.
>
> If this had been a jury trial or some other, it would have been grounds for a mistrial and possibly of contempt for the persons doing it . . . and those who have been doing it here are admonished to cease and desist from doing it. [There was no way for Harold to say the Sheriff had given him permission to sell the Blue Report in the courtroom; nothing for him but to "cease and desist" there in the front row, on the right.]

"Call your next witness," Moorman told the defense.

Cromwell, Kardy's assistant, was next. His testimony had to do with any seeming discrepancy in what Stella Watkins had said about how many of the boys had had intercourse with her. She had thought an emission was required; when it was explained to her that for legal purposes penetration alone was necessary, she amended her testimony to include all three.

The defense then rested its case. Kardy asked the three members of the Montgomery County police if he had ever told them to lie or whether he had in any way coached the witnesses, accepted their "No's," and called William Rogers to the stand.

The spectators shifted their positions and prepared to listen. It was now a little after three; the air-conditioning slightly tempered the heat of the July day, but the courtroom was stuffy. Judge Moorman's opening rebuke to Harold had roused them momentarily, but in those after-lunch hours they had drowsed back into inattention, bored with the questioning of the policemen, bored with the legalities of name, address, time, and place of service.

They looked closely at William, quietly dressed in a dark suit that was either new or freshly pressed. Kardy covered the same preliminary legalities and then went on to other questions having to do with whether he, Kardy, or any member of the police force had told him what to say on the stand. Then he asked, ". . . Specifically, Mr. Rogers, did you curse anyone at the scene and on the night of the rape?" No, Rogers had not.

Then Kardy made an abrupt and startling switch:

Q. Mr. Rogers, do you know Harold A. Knapp?
A. Very well.
Q. I will show you this man in the courtroom here and I will place my hand on him and ask him to stand. Do you recognize this man?
A. Very well.
Q. Who is that man?
A. Harold Knapp.
Q. Will you tell Judge Moorman, did there come a time this year when you had a conversation with Mr. Knapp?
A. Yes, there did.
Q. Would you relate to His Honor the circumstances under which you had the conversation?
Forer: Objection.
The Court: Overruled.
Q. Would you relate when and where you had that conversation and what that conversation was?
A. Well, first we talked over the telephone and he wanted to meet me . . . .

Forer again objected, and this time was upheld by Moorman, "unless," he said to Kardy, "you lay a proper foundation in order to establish the admissibility of the telephone conversation."

Kardy: We will proffer with Your Honor's permission respectfully that Mr. Knapp has contacted this witness on several occasions with the intent to get him to change his testimony, that he has bought him beer and whiskey on

several occasions, not only this witness but another witness
in the presence of this defendant here. After he has attempted to get this boy intoxicated so he would change his
testimony, that Mr. Knapp had this boy up in his house
in Germantown and gave him . . . and they drank ten or
fifteen drinks—the testimony will show that after drinking
these ten or fifteen drinks that Mr. Knapp tried to elicit
from this defendant facts in the Giles case, mentioned this
Hearing today, mentioned the depositions and tried to get
him to change his testimony while under the influence of
alcoholic beverages. We will also proffer to show that this
defendant will so testify that as a result of this dining and
drinking bout, Mr. Knapp was blowing bugles up there
in Germantown. He was swinging from trees in Germantown and also from this witness and corroborating witness,
this will be our proffer, that this man was tampering with
this witness, trying to get him to change his testimony.

Forer objected, but Moorman refused to strike the proffer:

I of course think we could have gotten along without much
of it, but what the State's Attorney has said in effect is that
a citizen has attempted to suborn perjury in a hearing
before a court.
Forer: What has that to do with this case?
The Court: That is a pretty serious thing. Just as we have
listened to the petitioners' allegation of subornation of perjury, now the State's Attorney . . . now I don't think Mr.
Forer, that the Court can wink away the State's question
that the State's Attorney gave. As a matter of fact I don't
know but that this is a question right now for the Grand
Jury on the statement of the State's Attorney alone. Now
this will not operate certainly against petitioners, I don't
think, as far as the record is concerned . . . . Now, you
may proceed Mr. Kardy to lay the foundation for the telephone conversation.

(For a moment before Kardy began again, there was an
almost palpable silence in the courtroom, "as though," said
Frances Ross, "we were all holding our breaths at the same
moment.")

Kardy: As a result of conversation you had with him, did Mr. Knapp come to see you?

A. Yes he did.

Q. Where did he come to see you?

A. The filling station on Route 1, Laurel.

· · · · ·

Q. Where did you go?

A. To a bar on Route 1 called the California Inn.

Q. Who was present at this bar, the California Inn on Route 1, besides yourself and Mr. Knapp?

A. Arnold Hawkins and he had another gentleman with him. I do not know his name.

Q. Do you see him in the courtroom today?

A. I don't think I would recognize him if I did see him.

Q. What time of day or night was it . . . ?

A. Around 9:00, 9:30.

Q. Did you have anything to drink?

A. Yes, we did.

Q. How much did you have to drink?

A. Quite a bit. Around six to seven drinks.

Q. How many drinks did Mr. Knapp have?

A. A couple.

· · · · ·

Q. Who paid for those drinks?

A. Mr. Knapp.

(The questions and answers were continually being interrupted by Forer's objections, most of which Judge Moorman overruled. The committee saw little point in this legal quibbling, but they realized that Forer was playing for time; he seemed edgy, tense, with every muscle taut).

Q. You may relate the conversation, Mr. Rogers.

A. Well, he started asking me about this case here . . . . Well, about the bathing suit and if I knew Stella's reputation before I went out with her and all this happened and I don't know, I can't remember everything. I started feeling pretty good there.

· · · · ·

157

Q. When did you next see Mr. Knapp after the California Inn?

A. 'Bout a month after that . . . . Around the same time . . . . He was by hisself.

Q. Were you with anyone?

A. Arnold Hawkins . . . . We proceeded toward his house.

Q. On leaving the station did Mr. Knapp offer you anything?

A. Yes, he had a jug of whiskey in the back of his car and he pulled it out and he had ice cubes and he fixed us all drinks . . . .

Q. Who was at his home when you got there?

A. His wife . . . .

Q. How much did you have to drink at his home?

A. I would say between ten and fifteen drinks . . . . He asked me the same questions. He asked me about did I call them ————— , and about the bathing suit and stuff like that . . . if you all put me up to saying anything that wasn't true . . . .

Q. How long were you up to his house?

A. I got home close to 4:00.

Q. And who did you come back with?

A. Arnold and Mr. Knapp and his wife.

Q. Who if anyone was blowing a bugle that night?

A. Mr. Knapp.

Forer: Object.

The Court: Well, what's the purpose of that, Mr. Kardy?

Kardy: I will withdraw that question.

Forer: May the record show I have a standing objection to this entire testimony regarding Mr. Knapp, because of the fact that the proper proof on the basis of which it was admitted shows absolutely no connection with the petitioners and this is entirely res inter olias acta.

Kardy: I don't know what that means . . . .

The Court: Yes, I know . . . .

Q. Did Mr. Knapp ever give you some strawberries?

A. Well, he gave me two boxes that night . . . he gave Arnie also a couple of boxes.

Q. Did Mr. Brooks, the witness that testified yesterday, did he tell you Mr. Knapp gave him $100 to testify?

. . . . .

A. Well, he told me Mr. Knapp gave him $100 to come down here to testify . . . .
Q. Did you have any conversation with a man named Mr. White about Mr. Knapp? About his testifying here in Rockville?
A. He told me Mr. Knapp gave him $12 yesterday and he'd give him the rest the next time he seen him . . . .

. . . . .

(At this point, one after another member of the press grabbed his belongings from the press box on the right and raced to a telephone booth to file his story. The next day the stories appeared with variations on the headline: KNAPP BRIBES WITNESS IN GILES CASE.)

The judge called a recess. Throughout that fifteen minutes, the committee stood against the walls out in the corridor, or went to get drink after drink from the water fountain. They said almost nothing. They all knew Harold's single-minded, dogged pursuit of all the "cruddy crowd." Some knew he had hoped to get William to sign the affidavit he had written; others did not. But they knew his passionate absorption in this case and suspected he might have bribed witnesses, feeling that the end justified the means.

If he had used those means, they felt their case was ruined.

XVI

After the recess, the spectators returned, but the press did not,
to hear Joe Forer cross-examine Rogers. He covered the same
ground Kardy had—the evening at California Inn, what
Knapp had asked, and what Rogers had answered—detailing
the conversation point by point. Then he wound up that evening and went on the next one.

Q. Was there any other thing said by Mr. Knapp on that
   occasion, in or on your way to the California Inn?
A. Not that I can remember.
Q. The fact is that anything that occurred after that you
   were in no position to remember?
A. That's right.
Q. Now, let's go to the house. That was a month later?
A. Yes.

· · · · ·

Q. Did you go willingly?
A. I went willingly . . . got in his car . . . he mixed a few
   . . . he had three tin cups, soda and ice in the car . . .
   took maybe an hour to get to his place . . . .
Q. Can you estimate how many ounces of whiskey you had
   in your first cup, or the second cup, or the third cup?
A. No, Arnie [Arnold Hawkins, his friend who worked at
   the gas station] mixed them. He was sitting in back.
Q. Were they pretty stiff?
The Court: Mr. Forer, what do you mean by stiff drinks . . .
   one of those country club little things?

[Forer asked Rogers, and ultimately the two agreed on double shots of 2–3 ounces each.]

Q. Now, when you got to the house, did you go inside?

A. First he showed me the swing and he got up and swang on it.

Q. Did you swing on it too?

A. I did.

Q. Did you, before you got on that swing, have a drink?

A. I told you I had two or three on the way.

Q. But now we are at the house and before you swung or swang, whatever the right word is—did you have a drink?

A. No.

Q. How long did you swing?

A. Don't know, swung on the thing one time and got off it. Felt like an idiot.

Q. You felt pretty good, didn't you? I mean, wasn't that the reason for your swinging?

A. I imagine so.

Q. This swing—did you have to climb a ladder to get onto it?

A. Yes, you did.

Q. As a matter of fact, the swing was about as high as this ceiling here, right?

A. Something like that.

Q. You climbed up this rickety ladder?

A. The ladder was only about ten feet. The rope was up in a tree about thirty feet.

Q. Did you go up the tree?

A. No, I didn't go up the tree.

Q. Did you go up to the top of the ladder?

A. Yes, I did.

Q. Did you stand on the top rung of the ladder?

A. I dunno. I know I stood on the top of it.

Q. Were you holding on to anything while you stood there?

A. Yes, on to the rope.

Q. Then you grabbed the rope and you took this long swing?

A. Right.

Q. How many feet was the arc?

A. I dunno.

Q. Then did you come back to the ladder or did you fall or what?

A. No, I came back. I drug my feet and got off of it . . . . I stopped it.

Q. Were you high?

A. I'd say I was high when I was on that rope.

(They had then gone into the house, been shown all around it, settled down for more drinks, and William admitted that shortly he was feeling "pretty good." Then they started talking about the Giles case, with Harold Knapp only asking him the same questions he had asked the night at the California Inn.)

Q. Then did there come a time when you'd had enough to drink so that you couldn't reliably testify as to what you said?

A. I guess there did. I passed out in the car that night.

Q. But until memory clouded, he just asked you the same questions? . . . And then you went home and you didn't see Mr. Knapp again until you saw him here in the courthouse?

A. Correct.

Q. No conversation by phone?

A. Correct.

Q. Did Mr. Knapp threaten you?

A. Nope.

Q. As a matter of fact you rather enjoyed the evening?

A. I would say I did.

Q. Did Mr. Knapp offer to pay you anything?

A. No.

Q. Now, before anything was said about the Giles case, you said Mr. Knapp gave you two boxes of strawberries— they were quarts, not crates?

A. Correct.

Q. Was anything said about their being given to you as a bribe to lie?

A. No . . . . I just said my wife liked strawberries . . .

Q. Now you said you spoke to Tom Brooks on Friday . . . . will you tell us again what Tom Brooks told you?

A. He told me that Mr. Knapp offered him $100 to come down here.

Q. Oh, now he said offered; he did not say "gave." Now which was it?

A. He said he offered him $100. I don't know whether he paid him or not . . . .

Q. Now was it paid or offered?

A. I dunno. All I know is what Tom told me . . . .

Q. Did he tell you he was stationed at Fort Monmouth?

A. Yes.

Q. Did he tell you the Army had given him a three-day pass to come down here for the purpose of testifying . . . . Did he tell you that Army regulations require that before they would give him a pass to come, that the people subpoenaing him or seeking to have his testimony had to agree to pay his expenses? Did he tell you that?

A. No, he didn't tell me that.

Q. Did he tell you what the $100 was for, other than what you told us now?

A. No, he didn't.

· · · · ·

Q. Let's take this business of Mark White and $12. When did you talk to him?

A. Last night?

Q. What time?

A. Around 8:30.

Q. Where?

A. At his home . . . .

Q. So you went over to see him to ask what was going on . . . what happened in court. What did he say to you?

A. Nothing much, said he got on the stand there and didn't know much more about it—he wasn't sitting here listening to it . . . . He didn't say no more, just said they had a subpoena out for me and I called Sargent . . . .

Q. He said who had a subpoena out for you?

A. The police.

Q. Did he tell you that he'd testified here for the petitioners, our side, the side I'm representing, the Giles brothers' side?

A. Not that I recall.

Q. So what else did you [and Mark White] talk about?

A. Nothing, he just told me Knapp paid him this $12 and said he'd give him the rest of it.

Q. Did he say what the $12 was for?

A. No, he didn't—just said Knapp said he'd give him the rest later. I guess he was beginning to pay for day's wages, as far as I know.

Q. What does Mark White do?

A. Plumber.

Q. Did he say the reason for this $12 was to reimburse him for lost wages?

A. Didn't exactly say that—just said Knapp gave him $12, said he'd give him the rest later. I don't know what he means by it . . . .

Q. Did you ask him why?

A. No, because I was curious about this warrant they had for me.

Q. You weren't curious about the $12? . . . Then how'd you come to mention it to Detective Collins?

A. Because Mark told me about it . . . .

Q. Then Detective Collins called you back at Mark White's?

A. Yes—they said stay where I was, they'd come pick me up. Gave me subpoena . . . said to be in court at 9:30 this morning. I told them I didn't think my car would make it, so they said I could stay there, in the police station . . . .

Then, at the police station he had given his testimony about Harold Knapp, read and signed the notes Detective Collins had taken down, and gone to sleep.

What followed in the courtroom, in the course of Forer's questioning showed how the tepid air and the pitch of emotions to which the afternoon had brought them had got on their nerves. Forer continued, his mind on those police notes William had signed:

Q. I ask that the State be required to produce—

Kardy: Here it is; put it in evidence. Be glad to.

Moorman: See what he wants to produce. You are antici-
pating him.

Forer: What I was getting ready to say before Mr. Kardy—

Moorman: Let him finish, Mr. Kardy.

Forer: I ask that the State produce both the handwritten
and typed notes that were taken at the time of the interview and interrogation of this witness.

Kardy: We have the typed notes here that are signed by
K. E. Collins, Detective Corporal; be glad to let you have
them if he offers them in evidence, glad to offer them in
evidence.

Forer: Your Honor—

Moorman: Just a minute, Mr. Kardy.

Forer: He is not permitted to interrupt.

Moorman: Just a minute. Let me say something. I'd like to
talk too, once in a while. Now you've made a motion—
#1, the typed notes, #2 the handwritten, I think you said
signed notes, didn't you?

Forer: Your Honor, if I may state my motion precisely . . .

Moorman: All right, now Number 1, you started to wave
something over there, Mr. Kardy. What was it?

Kardy: I have the typewritten notes that I would be glad
to have Mr. Forer have, if he introduced them in evidence.

Forer: May I be heard, Your Honor?

Moorman: Yes, but let me see . . . . Wait; your motion
about Mr. Kardy to produce . . . all right, I will hear you.

Forer: Your Honor, I am not asking Mr. Kardy for anything, by his grace, or anything on condition; I am asking
and I think I can ask it as a matter of right, in the light of
Jenks versus *U.S.*

Moorman: Mr. Forer, I will determine that . . . . Now Mr.
Kardy, you proferred him the handwritten notes, but—
wait a minute. Do you want to let him have it unequi-
vocally, no conditions on it?

Kardy: No, sir . . . . I proffer them if they are put in evidence . . . . We will proffer to Mr. Forer gladly, sir, both
handwritten and typed—

Forer: Please, Mr. Kardy. First of all, Your Honor, I am
not willing to take anything from Mr. Kardy as a matter
of grace on his part or subject to condition . . . .

The wrangling went on, until finally Judge Moorman cut in.

Let's get away from these personalities and stop this stupid talk with apologies. I say you [Forer] don't have to take anything from Mr. Kardy by his grace or by me or anybody else. What I am trying to do is to determine whether you are entitled to them. And now I don't think you are . . . It's a work product.

So Judge Moorman overruled Forer's motion, and continued.

Now, gentlemen, I mean no offense to either of you but you may get along a little further if you stop throwing these sarcastic motions to one another. I don't know whether you were justified, Mr. Forer. Mr. Kardy is a nice man; he doesn't mean some of the things he says. I've practiced against him and I used to want to throw him out the window. Let's stop it.

Forer: May I make a statement. I made a motion, Your Honor . . . which I still think is a good motion . . . Your Honor has ruled against me. I am not arguing further. Mr. Kardy interrupted my motion, started offering them on condition . . . I asked him not to interrupt . . . saying I was not ready to accept anything as a matter of grace or on condition . . . . It was a statement of my position and I do not understand why that should be regarded as being sarcastic to Mr. Kardy.

Moorman: Because you repeated about three or four times, Mr. Forer . . . . If I offended you, I am sorry, but not too sorry. But let's quit.

Forer: May I continue with the cross-examination?

Moorman: Yes, you may, you certainly may, by all means do.

Forer went over William's conversation with the police, eliciting nothing new, and then suddenly switched the subject.

Q.   Mr. Rogers, has anybody ever convicted you of a crime?
A.   Yes, I have . . . .
Q.   Once, or more than once?
A.   Once, as I recall.

Q. Once that you recall?
A. Yes, that's right.
Q. What was that one crime you recall being convicted of?
A. Petty larceny . . . .
Q. Where?
A. In Laurel.
Q. When?
A. Quite a few years ago.
Q. Other than that time have you ever been convicted?
A. As I remember, yes.
Q. That you remember?
A. I've been in a few fights . . . before . . . something like that . . . .
Q. Do you recall that on May 16, 1964 you were convicted in Odenton, Maryland . . . on a charge of destruction of property?
A. Yes I do.
Q. This conviction is not the one you remember happening several years ago, the petty larceny. That's a different one, yes?
A. Yes, it is.
Q. Do you recall on May 16, 1964 in Odenton you were charged with disturbing the peace?
A. I don't remember it.
Q. Well, perhaps I can refresh your recollection. This was a case on which the charge was brought on the oath of a man by the name of Edward Harrison, charging that on May 16, 1964 you disturbed the peace in violation of the law . . . . Don't you remember . . . you were convicted on three different charges.
A. I remember about the property part, the other ones I don't remember.

    . . . . .

Q. Do you remember the case tried March 7, 1961 . . . I'm sorry, I withdraw that . . . and that petty larceny charge you were found guilty of, that occurred on May 24, did it not? . . . Then there was a while back, back in '62. You were living in New Jersey, weren't you?
A. Might have been.

Q. You were arrested and convicted of a charge of bastardy? On July 13, 1962, weren't you?

A. I was arrested for it.

Q. And weren't you found guilty?

A. No, I wasn't.

Q. You weren't?

A. No, I don't think so.

Q. As a matter of fact, don't you make support payments now? Through the office of George Murphy, head of Gloucester County Probation Office, in New Jersey?

A. I don't make support to nobody.

Q. You were arrested . . . you admitted being the father of the child . . . . Do you remember you were ordered to pay $300 for medical payments and $10 weekly in support to a lady whose name I will not mention?

A. Nope, you're wrong. I paid $300 and that was it . . . no support . . . they put the baby up for adoption.

Q. Well, on May 24, 1960, on November 14, 1961 in the court of Hyattsville, Maryland, didn't you forfeit collateral on a charge of disorderly conduct by fighting?

Kardy: Just a minute—forfeiture is not a conviction.

Judge Moorman: Yes it is in Maryland, tantamount to a conviction.

A. I don't recall them charges . . . .

Q. You remember there were some but you don't remember . . . .

A. Sure there were.

Q. Quite a number?

A. You got them in front of you, don't you?

Forer listed two other forfeitures for disorderly conduct by fighting and then, for the next ten minutes, took William back over testimony he had given at the trials of the Giles and Joe Johnson, to the effect that he, Rogers, had not known anything of Stella Watkins's reputation for chastity, and had never discussed that reputation with anyone—not with Tom Brooks, Elston Finch, Eliot Jones, Evelyn Clark, whose affidavits contradicted what Rogers had said and was saying now. Forer had to struggle to ask these questions over Kardy's objections.

"I am trying to show that he testified falsely when he said he did not know the reputation of this girl . . . and that ties in with the fact that he told our witness, Tom Brooks, that the police had told him to give false testimony—play her up as a clean girl; coached to say he did not use that expression to the Negroes that I won't mention."

William Rogers remained obdurate: "I ain't heard anybody really discuss Stella Watkins and I ain't really discussed Stella Watkins to anybody."

Both Forer and Kardy were ready, finally, to let William go. Before he left Judge Moorman held him for a moment to ask if he had had his bathing suit that night. William was pretty sure he had it on, but he really didn't remember. He left the stand.

> The Court: Well, it's about 5:00 . . . . Do you have many witnesses on rebuttal . . . ? If we stay tonight it will be pretty late, won't it?

Forer had two witnesses, Tom Brooks and Evelyn Clark, waiting in the witness room. If they were not to be heard until the next day, Joe Forer wanted them instructed to remain.

> Forer: It's particularly important for Mr. Brooks because he is a private in the Army, and unless he is instructed to remain, the Army will raise all kinds of difficulties . . . .
> Judge Moorman: I was in the Navy for twenty-five years . . . probably give him a cup of coffee and shoot him. Well, now, is there any objection to recessing to tomorrow morning? We obviously can't finish without keeping very late hours, which is very hard on anybody . . . . I don't mind. I will stay here till 11:00, 12:00—hard on other people—just hurts my feet to stay here that long, but I can stand it.

The next morning Evelyn Clark testified that William Rogers's reputation for truthfulness was bad, and Tom Brooks testified to the same effect. Closing arguments by the lawyers followed and close to 11:00, on the morning of July 22, 1964,

Moorman dismissed the hearing with: "Right nice questions raised in here and I will be a considerable time digesting them after I get ahold of them."

On vacation in New England, ten days after the hearing, Harold Knapp wrote to the Brooks:

> The big thing I have discovered this week is a new and ter-
> rific sport. It's called sleeping. You do it in the sun; you do
> it in the shade. In bed and on the beach, day and night. It
> has a strange, intoxicating effect. It makes you feel better all
> over . . . .

XVII

Back from his vacation, Harold prepared for his trial on the suit brought by Mrs. Watkins for "disturbing the peace and disorderly conduct." He was taking no chances: if the police were capable of picking him up at ten at night to carry out an order given them by the sheriff seven days previously, anything could happen. He not only prepared a ten-page document telling how Mrs. Watkins had run out into the street to bang a bottle down on his Volkswagen, but lined up country neighbors, old friends, and a uniformed officer from the Pentagon, whose chest was covered with ribbons and medals, as character witnesses.

At the trial, none was called, nor was Harold himself. The only one to appear on the stand was Mrs. Watkins, earrings swinging: Harold, she said, had come past often in his VW, and as he paused for the stop sign, would race his engine and beep his horn once. She had brought no witnesses. The judge promptly dismissed the suit.

In November, after deliberating on the "right nice questions" raised at the post-conviction hearing, Judge Moorman handed down his decision. He ordered a new trial for the Giles, on the grounds that the State had "withheld from the defense and suppressed both the evidence concerning the second rape complaint of the prosecutrix and the evidence relative to her alleged suicide attempt and emotional disturbance . . ." He disallowed the claim that the State's witnesses had committed perjury with the knowledge of the State.

"To think that I voted against Judge Moorman because he was a Republican!" said Alice Alt.

"It was very courageous of Moorman," said Joe Forer. "His decision was almost unprecedented. I know of only one other such case. He put Maryland right up with the progressive states."

The committee was jubilant, but their joy was tempered first when Forer's plea to have the brothers out on bail was denied, and second when the State appealed to the Appeals Court of Maryland to reverse Moorman's decision. That the Appeals Court accepted the case for argument, Forer found foreboding. No longer jubilant, but still confident, the committee once again packed the red-carpeted courtroom in Annapolis, this time in April of 1965.

In July came the decision: Moorman's order for a new trial was reversed. "We hold that the evidence held by the lower court to have been suppressed was neither material to the guilt of the appellees, or to the punishment to be opposed, nor was the failure to disclose prejudicial to the accused. The non-disclosure, therefore, cannot be said to have amounted to the denial of due process." Two judges dissented, beginning their opinion with "The evidence admittedly withheld by the State could have been of vital importance to the defense of the accused, and its withholding constituted a violation of due process of the law."

The committee was stunned: how *could* the highest court in Maryland have reached such a decision? "Easily," said Joe Forer. "You don't realize what you've been doing. You're just a bunch of citizens, and you're interfering. You're fighting City Hall."

From the penitentiary John wrote: "The state of Maryland is as reluctant to let a innocent man go free, as a fox would be, in releasing a Rabbit he caught."

The next step, said Joe, would be to go again to the U.S. Supreme Court, which had previously refused to review the case on the grounds which Hal Witt had used in presenting it. The issue now would be the broad one of suppression of evidence by the State. Still, the Supreme Court might well refuse again.

A month after the Appeals Court decision, *Time* magazine ran an article on the case, with a picture of the Giles, entitled "A Girl's Reputation." It mentioned Stella by name. She promptly filed suit for a half-million dollars in damages. Harold supplied *Time*'s attorney with some ten pounds of documentary material, and mentioned the $3,000,000 suit against himself, Frances Ross, and Hal Witt. *"Time* should feel slighted," wrote Harold.

(A year later a New York judge dismissed the suit against *Time,* but the suit against the three in Montgomery County dragged on.)

XVIII

When they came off Death Row in the fall of 1963, the three prisoners were assigned jobs: John in the woodworking shop, James in the printing shop, and Joe Johnson in the metal shop, where Maryland's license plates were produced.

To be again with other human beings, and to feel that life was once more an ongoing process, were at first exhilarating sensations. Then tedium took over, and it bothered John the most, for he had been put to sanding wood. He asked for a transfer, claiming that he was allergic to the dust sanding produced. He was probably allergic, in reality, to the boring, repetitive nature of the task, as the penitentiary officials no doubt suspected. They refused to transfer him, and put him on "correction"—loss of good-conduct credits. The action had no effect on John, and in the end the officials gave in, and let him change to making furniture.

James was from the beginning content with his job, because he learned new skills in the printing shop which would be useful in the outside world. Joe hated his and tried to get transferred to the upholstery shop, but never succeeded in doing so.

Harold wrote the three of them more often than did anyone else on the committee. Though writing was easy for him, he frequently had to force himself to the chore when he wanted to get to bed and sleep. He kept them informed of every stage of their case and also the civil ones, of what was going on in the

Knapp family, and of what he felt free to tell them about the research he was doing. He lectured them from time to time on making the most of their enforced time, but always followed the lecture with a quick apology for sounding moralistic, or with a touch of whimsy.

If that whimsy—by which they knew him long before they met him—baffled them in the beginning, there was no question as to its effect on the prison censor, who took his queries to the officials. They found nothing harmful in something like the following:

> I forgot to tell John that a mother quail chose to make a nest and hatch 7 eggs in the tall grass about 30 feet in front of our front windows. We were in mortal terror for her every time a dog wandered by. But she survived and hatched the little birds and they were scarcely 2 days old when she marched them all off into the big, wide world. Hopefully they all grow up to be prosperous, rich and happy. And law abiding. Can't stand disorderly quails.

But they disapproved when Harold wrote:

> Now, finally . . . I am coming back to life on several fronts and particularly to pick up again the Giles-Johnson case. Perhaps you remember that case. Back in 1961 B.C. there was this here girl, and a State's Attorney and a Judge, and a fine young man named William Rogers, and three bad people named Flopsie, Mopsie and Cottontail, John, James and Joseph, who went down the lane to pick gooseberries and ended up in Mr. Finan's penitentiary . . . .

They also disapproved of his writing to the prisoners as though they were innocent.

Frances Ross and Reverend Mason went to meet the prison officials one day and got an implacably hostile reaction to the subject of Harold Knapp.

"He's making these young men think they're some kind of heroes. Every man in this prison thinks he's innocent. We don't like to encourage it. This man Knapp's not only a nut, he's a bad influence."

"You just don't understand Dr. Knapp," said Frances Ross. "He's a very fine man. If you met him, you'd agree."

The officials did not want to meet him, and for some time they forbade the boys to write to him and returned his letters unopened. Harold had met opposition before; he met it now by writing a most humble, chastened letter to the warden, asking what mistakes he had made, how he should have written, and so on. In a flanking movement, he organized the committee to follow his lead and wire the state legislature to vote more funds for the penitentiary, a fact he mentioned to the warden. Shortly thereafter, he was reinstated as a correspondent, and in time was permitted to visit the boys, as were the other committee members.

The period during which letters in both directions were forbidden was a distressing one for the Giles, and presumably for Joe Johnson, who often requested to be in "lockup" and was thus unseen by the Giles. They were in another period of depression when John wrote:

> I still have hope that we will win . . . . I have always been told that the truth is the most powerful thing in this world, and with that I plan to win—or die trying . . . . I will just try to make the best of this mess . . . I will Just get my self a Job—outside in the yard, or outside some where—if possible, eat lots of state food, be nice to everybody, be as active as possible—in as many sports as possible, go to church as often as I can, write my family and friends as much as possible . . . and die heart-stricken if they don't release me from this place soon.

And James wrote:

> I write tonight in a much better frame of mind than I've been in for days. If I sometimes write and sound as though

> I'm flat and empty, it's because I'm in the dumps. From time
> to time I become depressed, even though I try all I know how
> not to . . . all at once I get my mind all tied up in a lot of,
> I suppose, silly things.

The committee responded promptly: might inmates receive
newspapers or magazines? Yes, answered James, and added,
"We are very limited in reading material; in fact I have not
read a newspaper in months and magazines only when I can
persuade someone to part with them." The committee subscribed to the *Montgomery County Sentinel, Life* and *Field
and Stream* for John; the *Washington Post, Star* and *News-
week* for James; the *Post* and *Look* for Joe Johnson. These
helped.

Letters from the outside helped most of all and imposed on
the Giles (only occasionally on Joe) the discipline of answering them. They had written letters rarely in their lives.
Through the need to do so now, plus the interest the committee took in them, the prison experience became very much one
of growing and emerging. John's interests did not broaden beyond his focus on "nature," but his intelligence quickened;
James's both quickened and broadened under the stimulus.

They wrote in their 7 x 8½ foot, steel-walled cell which,
like most of the others in the old, labyrinthine fortress, had to
house two men because the prison population had almost
doubled (from 900 to 1500) since it was built in 1803 and
enlarged in the 1890's. The walls of their cell were painted a
pale green; a naked bulb in the ceiling lighted it; the only shelf
was not more than a foot long, so they stored their boxes of
letters, keepsake albums, and the books that were sent them
under their double-decker bunks. The cell had no room for a
chair, so they wrote lying down or sitting on their bunks.

John, after his early informative letters about the events of
the night on Batson Road, and about his own life, wrote most
freely about "nature," and a bond developed between him and

Harold on this subject, although Harold was selective in his allegiance, and John was not.

John wrote Harold specifically, more than once, about how to feed and care for the black snake which had made its appearance close to the house on the ridge. Harold should provide it with live birds; he should catch field mice and only gradually accustom the snake to becoming a household pet. It really would not need a meal of mice and birds more than once a week. In time, mention of the black snake disappeared from Harold's letters; but from John's, it took longer.

> . . . . Today, a Sunday, I decided to do something different for a Change, I smoked five salem filter cigarrettes stayed in bed late and ate all the good food I could get hold of and didn't do anything active all day, now that it's late and I am locked in my cell I feel very energetic but theres not much to do now, what a nut I am sometimes!
>
> I am very glad to hear that you caught gordon the five foot black snake, but sorry to hear he got away two times because they make very nice pets, have you caught him again yet? do you have any live food to feed him? because they usually won't eat anything else. They had two snakes here at the pen school for a long while but they don't have them any longer which makes me very mad because I use to go see them quite often, one was a King snake, the other a milk snake . . . .

"Gordon" disappeared from Harold's letters, but he often referred to various wild creatures he met while clearing brush, or when they appeared in the light out on the terrace. John picked up each mention and enlarged on the habits of the creature in question: "It is not necessary to slit the tongue of a crow to get it to talk." "I am glad your racoon has become a regular evening visitor because they are a very interesting animal." "Right now I'm doing some study on mammals. Did you know that Bats are the only known flying mammals of today?"

Much later he wrote,

> I have a pet turtle [he got it from the science class at the
> penitentiary, to which he did not belong] which is very tame.
> I will have a picture of her taken also, whenever it's possible.
> I like turtles much better than fish and find them very inter-
> esting in various ways.

In the woodworking shop John found some sickly plants,
which he took over and "fixed up" so successfully that a prison
official brought him seeds and soil. He planted tomatoes in
metal buckets set in the catwalk outside the shop, and soon
was growing flowers in cardboard boxes, food tins, and any
other container he could get his hands on. He experimented
with orange and grapefruit seeds salvaged from the dining hall
(plants but no fruit); he tried to make a green curtain out
of morning glories for the windows of the science room at
the prison school (cloth curtains were not permitted lest the
inmates tear them up to make escape ropes). In time he was
given a janitorial job in the prison school; it paid less than
woodworking, but gave him more time to fuss with the plants
and the beds of flowers he was permitted to grow out in the
yard.

His flowers earned him a spell of local fame. A major event
at the prison was a show put on in the yard by an outside
group including *The Platters,* a group of recording stars "with
10 gold records."

> Before the show started, [John wrote Harold] I cut a pretty
> bouquet of some of the flowers I grew and gave them to the
> pretty female singer . . . she was very pleased and gave me a
> great big kiss and a picture with her autograph. Many in-
> mates were pleased by this, also, and have been calling me
> lover and ect. all day long. Now I am very sorry I didn't take
> her the whole flower bed.

He started school in the prison, but soon stopped.

> I changed my mind about going to school. I have found
> that I do much better doing personal studies than having
> someone teach me and I want to learn as much as possible
> about as many things as possible, but I want to learn best the
> things I am most interested in . . . about plants . . . . I have
> the feeling of being free and easy when I am growing plants.

A subcommittee of the Giles-Johnson Defense Committee set
up correspondence courses for all three. Since John had not
finished seventh grade, he worked for a certificate rather than
credit, taking such courses as *Soil Fertility and Management,*
Propagation of Plants, and *Bulbs for Your Flower Garden.* He
would read the manuals, then fill out and return the test
papers. "He only reads those manuals once," wrote James,
ruefully, "and he knows what's in them, and gets all A's and
Excellents!"

After the serious prison riot in the summer of 1966, all the
inmates were locked in their cells for ten days with radio, TV,
newspaper and magazine privileges withdrawn. The tempera-
ture outside was in the mid-90's. "On it goes," wrote James,
"so far nothing has changed. From where we sit, locked in
our cells, it's hot! Stifling. We read most of the day and say
very little. We agree that the heat makes us irritable."

All John cared about during the rioting was his flowers.

> When I first saw a couple of people walking in my flowers,
> my thought was to go over and hit someone in the mouth, but
> shortly a dozen or so were in them, so I changed my mind
> about trying to save them because somebody could have been
> hurt, most likely me.
>
> I fear my flowers are done for, [he wrote later] and I'm
> very sorry I can't save them because it's taken almost three
> years of my spare time to grow them all . . . those inside will
> die, too, because I can't water them . . . . I will be glad when
> this cleans up and I can get out of this cell, being inactive
> kills me.

The officer who first arranged for him to grow flowers in the yard tried to get him out of his cell to care for them now, but without success. John himself wrote to the warden during those ten days asking permission to "fix the flowers that were hurt." The request was not answered.

Finally John could write:

> Good news! one, I went back to work today and now I feel great. Two, my flowers inside look better than ever, thanks to a couple of kind and thoughtful people who likes flowers. You can't imagine how happy I am about this.

While they were still on Death Row, Harold had suggested to James that he write a book, and the idea became for him a focus of his thoughts and dreams. It continued to be after he joined the prison population. First it was to be a novel; he sketched its outline and began to accumulate notes. Then he planned a book on his own experiences, and what had brought him to prison. The planning in itself helped him to objectify his situation.

> Let me also point out that I myself do not hope to get out of here without serving some time because I rightly should. In my brother's case, this wouldn't be looked on in the same light, because he is completely innocent of any disorderliness, but as it stands we are here for a crime that very definitely was not committed . . . the wrong I am guilty of [smashing the car window] and am willing to pay for has been literally ignored.

And he saw that had Judge Pugh given them twenty years, or life imprisonment instead of the death sentence, "the State would not only have achieved its objective but the facts of the case would have been obscured to the public."

The prison had a course in creative writing which he took, and later another in the same subject by correspondence. His vocabulary and grammar improved although some old habits persisted: "helt" for held, and at decreasing intervals the Negro idiom: "the things he say and the things he do." Always more articulate than John, he grew steadily more so—and more natural—with the discipline of writing.

> At the moment everything is going along at its usual pace. Joe is still in the hospital (a broken leg from baseball) John is still growing anything that will grow and I—well, I'm doing nothing right now but reading books halfway through before putting them aside never to be finished. You might say I'm at a point where I have trouble getting interested in things.

He wrote that letter during one of the many periods of waiting for a decision to be announced, in this instance that of the Appeals Court. When the decision came he went back to "finishing the half-read books I laid aside before the Court's ruling."

Marie Ferington of the committee and her husband began to send books to the prisoners through Mr. Grey, the head of the prison school, who had to look them over first to make sure no coded messages had been written in. John's requests were usually for books on plants or animals, Joe Johnson's for current best-sellers; but James's choices were eclectic: Kafka, Dostoevsky, *Walden, Looking Backward*.

When the committee set up courses for John, they set up others for James and Joe. James elected to try College Freshman English, offered by Penn State University. He was first given a diagnostic test.

> I now have the results of the English pre-test and as I had already predicted, my score did not meet—or did not show that I could meet the standard of English usage at Penn State. But fortunately the form letter notified me that my low score would not prevent me from taking English I. Naturally, to have flunked from the outside is a somewhat nasty experience, but I'm not about to sit around brooding over it. The thing to do now is to take the challenge.

He took up other challenges, too.

I didn't mention it in my last letter, but I've been having a sort of vacation. Many of us who before worked in the Print Shop now spend all day doing nothing in the way of work. We just go to the yard, read or play checkers and chess or do other such things to occupy time. This has been going on for more than three weeks—no, it's been over a month—but it's about to come to an end now that reconstruction work on the print shop is almost completed.

Other than doing just a little more than routine reading, I used this free time to loaf. I justify doing nothing by telling myself the English course will start soon and that I'll be continually busy once it does . . . . As for prison courses, I started Spanish this week . . . . Now I'm back from my first Espanol leccion and it's late and the lights will soon go out . . . so this will be short . . . . When the Spanish class was over I had an hour to kill so I sat in on the Business Administration class. I thought it was interesting and for that reason I enrolled. The time for hard work is suddenly and definitely here.

. . . We are able to study in the evenings after the work day is done, either in the cell or on the nights there are classes held, in the school. There is, however, no place where I could have access to for quiet study. That there is never a quiet moment, except in the wee hours of the morning when all the prison is asleep, accounts largely for the statement I made some time ago that prison is perhaps the worst place in the world to take on the study of anything. Of course after a while, one becomes accustomed to constant noise and study can be accomplished if the mind is disciplined to the task. But it is not an easy task.

. . . My days pass in a blur. From the time I get up till "lights out" I get as much done as possible. Today something extra. I was up before the first bell sounded and worked an hour or more on this week's assignment for the correspondence course; then to breakfast and back to the cell to finishing a book I had hated to lay aside in the first place. The book got finished, then back to work on the assignment. By 12:30 I counted more than a 1000 words, but wasn't satisfied when proofing, so I rewrote the whole thing. I liked it then; it sounded better. I enveloped and stamped it and got it out of the way. Then I wrote a letter to a friend and one to my sister, too. Read a 100 pages in *House of the Dead*. It was then about 6:00 P.M. and time for the final meal. Came back from the dining hall, washed a sweat shirt, made a peanut butter sandwich (I'm developing a strong dislike for peanut butter) ate that along with an orange, terrible things to eat together. Read some more of *House of the Dead,* remembered I hadn't yet answered your last letter. Decided to put it off till tomorrow. Changed my mind and here, Mr. Knapp, this lunacy . . . can it be called a letter?

That's the way all my days have been going for more than a month now. Can you believe that I'm happy when I fill such a schedule? It makes me sleep well, too.

The college-level English correspondence course remained James's major challenge. At times its requirements—especially those for "Exposition"— were difficult to fulfill, assuming, as they did, access to a good library. The penitentiary had a library, but most of the books were old novels with a sprinkling of outdated textbooks. No card catalogue existed, so James had to wander from shelf to shelf, hoping that on one he might find the factual material he needed.

In spite of flunking the diagnostic test, he got an A in the course. Both the committee and he began to think in terms of college when he got out. He lacked algebra, science, social studies, and history. He had been interested only in sports in high school, and studied only enough to get grades which were barely passing. His teachers had advised him to take the "commercial" courses, and he accepted the advice without question. Nor did his parents quibble with his high school major: "Dry-Cleaning." They were proud to have him get a high school diploma, regardless of which subjects he took to earn it. "Truth, honesty, manners—those were what I was brought up to think important," said their great-uncle, Caleb Adams. And these, plus a narrow, literal religion, were what

Mary Giles had tried to pass on to her sons. Books to read, talk of what was going on outside the small world of the Batson Road community, were nonexistent.

The odds were against any college's taking him, but the committee continued to explore possibilities and James continued to study and write letters such as the following, whose subject matter and treatment alike would have been impossible for him five years before:

> Dear Mrs. Ferington,
>
> I have your letter of May 3; as always, I was glad to hear from you. Yes . . . I now have Plato's *Republic,* and *Basic History: United States.* Dylan Thomas's *Under Milkwood* has not come yet, thought *J.B.* was great; also, as you suggested I read Job in the Bible for comparison. Completely apart from what Job is ment to demonstrate, it seems to me that *J.B.* captures so much of the absurdity and inevitability of events. And, although the course and order of things are set, I was nevertheless left with the feeling while moving with Nick and Mr. Zuss that there ought to have been a solution to break the absurdity and inevitability of Job's plight, of what was in store for him, for all of humanity. But in his absolute aloneness, J.B. cannot curse God to his face and die; the order of things is set and to reject faith is of no consequence. I know the intent of Job is not to show that what is built up in life is comparable to building a house with the knowledge that it will and must burn down; yet it suggests that, but not that faith won't save it either; the house will burn notwithstanding that, and Job is restored to wait till next time around.
>
> I am now well into *The Proud Tower.* I must admit that it is not the cut-and-dried type of book I had expected it to be; rather it is not only tremendously informative, but also enjoyable. I like it so much that, sometime later, may I please have *The Guns of August,* also?

John and James saw very little of Joe Johnson. Either he was in a distant cell in another part of the penitentiary or—as became almost a permanent situation—in "lock-up." "Lock-up" meant solitary confinement, with meals on trays, and any prisoner might request it, as Joe Johnson did. He was intensely nervous and volatile; being in lockup relaxed him.

His position was a difficult one in any event. Since his trial had been in a separate county, a year later, the fate of his case was contingent on that of the Giles. He was always peripheral, and was even headlined in a newspaper as the "Third Giles Figure." It was the Giles who got out of the penitentiary to look at the outside world—three days for the post-conviction hearing, one day for this, another for that—not Joe.

He was well aware of the difference and also aware, when committee member Lew Maddocks came to talk to them about their studying, that John could report A's on his tests, and James how many phases of his Freshman English course he had completed; whereas he, Joe, had been held up on his correspondence courses for lack of a text, or lack of time, or . . . Only the completion of two courses remained between him and his high school diploma, still . . .

Early in his years at the penitentiary, the committee arranged for him to be fitted with false teeth, which he had long needed and which raised his morale. Also, he became healthier as the prison routine wore on, and complained less of headaches. Harold never established the rapport with Joe that he had with the Giles, but he kept on trying. Whether his letters were answered or not, he cajoled, talked of chess (which Joe played skillfully when not in lockup) or baseball, or tried to inject some degree of self-discipline into Joe. The answers were guarded and infrequent—Joe was always running out of stamps.

Relations between the committee members and the prison officials were at last good enough for Mr. Grey, the head of prison education, to let Lewis Maddocks, Marie Ferington, and Sam Legge—a Baltimore Quaker who had become interested in the case—see the prisoners at the penitentiary almost any time they wished. The three committee members constituted a subcommittee for "Education and Readjustment." Mr. Grey would meet them at the front door and take them to an empty office in one of the subterranean rooms. There, chaperoned only by a stout guard who was inclined to doze, the three boys would sit on one side of a booth, the committee on the other (so disposed lest the visitors slip something to the prisoners) and talk with freedom. John's face, ordinarily sad, would literally pucker with merriment when he was about to say something funny, or merely personal. "Wherever plants grow all year round, there's where you'll find me when we get out of here." But he spoke little, partly from shyness, partly because the other two did not give him much chance. James's responses to questions or ideas were so quick, given with a lift of the head, that he seemed all openness, in contrast to John.

Though Joe had filled out somewhat in prison, he remained slender, his face pointed, his eyes large and lustrous. He liked to talk even more than James did and he was even more articulate, having an exceptional command of words. He had sent Mrs. Ross several poems, an outpouring of emotions with end rhymes which she thought at first he might have copied from some book of "Uplift Verse." "No," said his father, "he's always written verse on occasions which moved him." When his textbook for senior high school English finally arrived, he worked at it with an enthusiasm he could not summon for algebra. He liked *Beowulf* and *Piers Plowman* ("once you get the beat, you like it"); preferred Browning to the Romantics. He had written, while still on Death Row,

> Another thing that bothers me, is in finding something in which to further the advancement of our community. Because what is really lacking among us is versatility in music,

> Sports, and Reading . . . since I have been here I was intro-
> duced to such composers as Henry Mancini, Mario Lanza,
> Beethoven . . . .

The subcommittee found him immensely likable as he
talked across the table in the windowless room. But the courses,
alas, remained unfinished.

Joe Forer had filed his petition for certiorari (the means of
bringing a case up from a lower court to the U. S. Supreme
Court) in October, 1965. Maryland ignored it until the Supreme Court called for a response in January of 1966. Maryland then asked for an extension of time to prepare a response,
and so the uncertainty dragged on.

Harold was careful to warn the prisoners: the Supreme
Court took only an average of 150 such petitions out of the
2500 or so it received every year. The Supreme Court would
accept their petition only if it involved constitutional decisions
it found new or significant.

"Everything seems to be taking an awful long time," wrote
James. "Patience, patience, patience. Fortunately ours have
developed into the best around."

At the end of March, he wrote:

> WOW!
> We came into the cell this evening. Tired. In an ill-humor.
> This day had not been the best. Then it came, on the
> 4:00 P.M. newscast, catching us completely off guard and
> we exploded, literally, as if we had just gone mad. Whoopie!
> We had taken your advice and had not gotten our hopes
> up that the Court would act on the petition today, the 21st;
> so when it came you can imagine our reaction. Thank heavens
> for the federal Court system, especially the Supreme Court.
> And now, indeed, we'll take the world as it comes and beat
> it as soon as we can, by golly.

XIX

"With Joe Forer and justice on your side," Harold once wrote the Giles, "the ultimate outcome is certain enough. What we don't know is just when or how it will come about."

His putting Forer first was deliberate. Along with the rest of the committee he was beginning to lose faith in the judicial system; none of them lost faith in Joe Forer.

Most other lawyers would long since have dropped the case, if only because they could not afford the continuing investment of time without financial return. Forer could not afford it either, but he went ahead regardless. He lengthened his working day to add this case to his other legal commitments, and worked in the evening when he would have preferred to be reading—"I read everything; in fact, if I can't read I get jittery."

Representing the Giles and Johnson involved far more than preparing and presenting arguments. He had for clients the entire committee, who telephoned him for advice, turned over to him anything they wrote to be checked for libel, and, in critical stages, brought him away from his home six nights out of seven for meetings which were often discursive and time-wasting. With a mind that was quicker than most, he was not a naturally patient man, but he remained patient with the committee and its ignorance of the law.

Besides handling the Giles-Johnson criminal case, he handled the civil ones brought against Harold, and the $3,000,000 one against Harold, Frances Ross, and Hal Witt, which went through so many legal vagaries and postponements that they agreed it was a toss-up whether it or the criminal case would be decided first. And always Forer had to cope with the continuing barrage of letters from Harold, each packed with new ideas to be explored, new angles to be looked into, or new suggestions for affidavits they might try to get.

The committee was able to meet the financial obligations of making transcripts and reimbursing witnesses for time and travel expenses; of having briefs printed and petitions mimeographed. (Nancy Feldman, treasurer of the committee, mailed the clerk of the Supreme Court a check for $2,445 to cover printing and clerical work necessary for the appeal.) When all these demands had been met, not much was left in the treasury. What there was, they sometimes persuaded Joe Forer and Hal Witt to take. More frequently, Forer would say, "Better wait; we have lots of things coming up which will take money." But no committee, however skilled at fundraising, would have been able to compensate him adequately for the endless man-hours he dedicated to trying to win freedom for the prisoners.

He marshaled his thoughts quickly, but shaping them on paper was a different matter. He had been a prize-winning Latin student at Rutgers, and had taken an M.A. in English literature before studying law. He cared about good prose, and in his pleasant, unpretentious office he wrote and rewrote, swinging from desk to typewriter and back, changing and polishing his sentences. As the years passed he wrote, or told, the story of what had happened on Batson Road—the "Criminal Proceedings"—to the point of his own tedium. Yet he would pick up the recital again, from the moment the boys stopped fishing until they were sentenced to death, treat it with scrupulous objectivity, and by the very dryness with which he told the lurid events of that night, invest them with a heightened drama.

No more than in a post-conviction hearing was the major question for the Supreme Court that of innocence or guilt. Forer had to persuade the Court that the Giles-Johnson case was one "whose resolution will have immediate importance far beyond the particular facts and parties involved," as Chief Justice Vinson had once said.

"We're making a mountain out of a molehill," said Joe to the committee. "Still, it's a pretty good molehill."

In his certiorari petition, and later in his brief, it was the same mountain: that the State, through its agents, had known facts which might have cleared the boys of guilt if the defense had known them.

> . . . This case presents major issues concerning the meaning and application of the doctrine that prosecution suppression of exculpatory evidence is a violation of due process which vitiates a conviction. These issues have never been resolved by this Court. Indeed, the Court has barely touched on the doctrine which—unlike other advances in criminal jurisprudence—has been developed by State and lower federal courts. This grass-roots development indicates that the doctrine is a necessary response to advancing demands for the fair administration of criminal justice and for a reduction of the handicaps of impoverished defendants.

The Supreme Court, in the Brady case in 1963, had decided it was a violation of due process to suppress evidence favorable to the accused whether the prosecution had acted in good or bad faith. But there was a joker in that decision, to the effect that it was a violation only if the accused asked for such evidence. Lower federal courts had frequently decided that "upon request" was not necessary to prove suppression. Joe Forer pleaded that point: "The need for disclosure is greatest precisely when the defense is so unaware of the exculpatory evidence as not to know what, or even whether, to demand." For example, Kardy had handed Stedman Prescott his file on the Giles case. Why would Prescott "request" a disclosure?

> Because of the social importance of the suppression doctrine, because its development without illumination from this Court has been uneven and incomplete, and because its uncertainties are recurring, we believe that it is time for the Court to contribute its guidance in this field on the first appropriate occasion.
>
> This case is that occasion. The issues involved are basic to the suppression doctrine . . . . This case—often called the Little Scottsboro Case—has raised extensive doubt about our system of criminal justice. These doubts will not be allayed short of this Court's review . . . .

The Maryland Appeals Court had decided, in reversing Moorman, that neither Stella's suicide attempt nor the second rape charge was "material," and hence did not violate due process.

> What is the standard [asked Forer] for determining whether undisclosed evidence is "material"? Is materiality determined merely by what the prosecution knew, or also what the defense would have discovered if the prosecution had disclosed what it knew? Whose knowledge constitutes knowledge of the "prosecution"? Is the prosecution charged not only with its actual knowledge but also with the constructive knowledge it would have discovered by rudimentary diligence?

He went on to write of the information Harold Knapp had dug out and which—if the State had not known—it could have found out except for "gross negligence."

Wasn't failure to investigate to be blamed on the prosecution —when such investigation might help the indigent accused who had no resources to conduct such an investigation? Even if suppression of vital facts was not deliberate on the part of the State, was it not still responsible for failure to follow up such palpable leads as it had been given, even if Stedman Prescott knew nothing of them?

> Yet the State's Attorney and the police did not lift a finger [to inquire] into Stella's record and character [or to] attempt to verify the account of the accused by checking whether she was "on probation." They maintained their lethargy even after they had received the further startling news of the attempted suicide and the second rape accusation . . . . In short, the State's Attorney and the police . . . determinedly rejected exposure to information favorable to the accused despite the suspicious circumstances surrounding the accusation. It is unbelievable that they would have shown the same apathy if the social and economic status of the protagonists had been reversed—if the accused had been white, middle-class youths and the complaining witness an impoverished Negro girl.*

His plea for the Court to review the case was sixty-four pages long, plus an index and the citation of seventy-five cases. Five months passed before the Court announced its decision to review. Was that decision unanimous or had only the required four voted to review? The weekly conferences of the Court were held in total secrecy. There was no possible way of knowing.

The arguments began on the morning of Wednesday, October 12, 1966. Few of the committee members had heard a case argued in that courtroom before, and they were surprised by the contrast between the formality of the room—Ionic marble columns, huge brass open-work gates, dark-red velvet curtains—and the complete informality with which the hearing was conducted.

There facing them was seventy-five-year-old Chief Justice Warren, keystone of the nine, who, in the daily routine of admitting lawyers to practice before the Court, played the role of gracious host: smiling, avuncular. Justice Black sat on

* *Brief for Petitioners*, p. 37.

his right, eighty now, and looking so waxen, so fragile, that it seemed amazing that he could withstand the demands of the courtroom day. Farther to Warren's right sat sixty-seven-year-old Justice Clark, soon to leave the Court, Justice Brennan, sixty, and Justice White, forty-nine, who often rocked his large leather chair back and forth, or swiveled it to murmur something to Brennan.

To Warren's left was Justice Douglas, sixty-eight, of whom the spectators could see little except a shock of gray hair, for he asked no questions and never looked up except to ask his page for another book to add to those behind which he was writing. ("Douglas almost never looks up," said Forer. "That's just the way he is.") On Douglas's left was Justice Potter Stewart, looking far more youthful than his fifty-one years, and lastly Justice Abe Fortas, fifty-six, farthest on the left in the spot reserved for the newest member of the Court. (The man who would next occupy that spot, Thurgood Marshall, listened to the arguments that day from one of the few seats reserved for honored guests or members of the bar.)

Joe Forer, representing the side which had lost in the lower court, began the argument. He was poised and even more quiet than usual. His only gesture was an occasional lift of a hand in emphasis, or the removal of his glasses. "Mr. Chief Justice, and may it please the Court . . . " and he spoke along the lines of his brief.

The Justices were clearly listening, except for Douglas, who had learned the art of listening and writing simultaneously. From time to time they broke in, so that the occasion seemed more of an intimate dialogue than it did in a lower court. From the questions asked, the committee guessed at what the Justices were thinking. Brennan seemed in agreement; at least his questions were never negative. They served, as did those of Abe Fortas, to clarify and strengthen the points Forer was making. Warren seemed to be going along as well, showing particular concern over a possible new trial and whether the boys knew it might go adversely.

The committtee did not have to guess at Justice Black's position. He asked Forer legal question after question, interrupting him before he could finish his answer until Forer's annoyance was clear. ("I admire Black more than any other Justice. In all the cases I've argued in that court, he's always been on my side," said Forer. "I was upset.")

When Black asked, "Had the girl ever before had relations with colored men?" the committee as well as Forer knew he was lost. (Potter Stewart asked the same question, but his worried them less.)

As to Harlan? No knowing. White? Probably agreeing with Forer. Clark? He gave no clue. Nor did any come from the bent head of Douglas.

Then the State began to argue, in the person of the Assistant Attorney General, Donald Needle. He was youthful, attractive, and appeared uneasy. His uneasiness grew as his hour for argument wore on, as the questions from the bench multiplied, and as several of the Justices seemed no longer to be listening. His argument was broken by a half hour for lunch, but matters for him did not improve once he had resumed.

The State's Attorney for Montgomery County could not be held responsible, he said, for what was going on in another county, namely, Stella's run-ins with the juvenile court of Prince George's County. Furthermore, as the Court had ruled in *Brady,* unless the defense had requested disclosure of evidence, the prosecution was not at fault for suppressing that evidence. Stedman Prescott had made no "request."

"We say," he continued, "that the Fourteenth Amendment does not demand as broad an interpretation as the defense demands."

Neither the Maryland Court of Appeals nor the Rules of Maryland had taken such a broad stand.

"Why did her parents want her on probation?" Warren broke in.

Needle hedged. He had not read the reports from the juvenile courts; he did not know her parents had wanted her on probation.

"You may consult counsel," said Warren.

Needle consulted counsel, but the counsel beside him at the table did not know either. They had not read the record nor brought it with them.

"I want to *know*," repeated Warren.

Black cut in. "You started to tell us what happened that night. You mean the defendants broke into the car because they thought Rogers was going to shoot them? Or because William Rogers shouted racial epithets?"

Needle was unsure of this point and played for time until Warren interrupted him with, "You've answered both 'yes' and 'no.' You must decide which."

Needle could not decide.

"Suppose the State," asked Abe Fortas, "then knew what we now know, would the State then have been obliged to divulge what it knew?"

"Well," said Needle, "those facts might have been useful . . . but utility by itself is not enough. The prosecution was not required by Maryland's rules to disclose what they had discovered."

Warren rephrased Fortas's question: "Do you think that in order to have a fair trial the State should have disclosed what it knew?"

"No, sir, considering the information then available, nothing prevented a fair trial."

"If the judge," Warren persisted, "had known the facts the prosecution knew, wouldn't he have taken into consideration something less than death, even down to the point of eighteen months, which I understand is permissible sentence for rape under Maryland law?"

"Under moral obligation, not a constitutional one, the evidence might have been offered the judge," said Needle. "It's a moot question."

"You can't call that moot," said Warren, tartly.

"Did they weigh everything?" Warren continued. "The State had information it did not disclose. Should that information not have been given, if not for the trial, at least for the sentencing? . . . The fact that we do know it now, shouldn't the defendants have it . . . so they don't spend the rest of their lives in jail?"

"Well," said Needle, "the Appeals Court did have the information and reversed Moorman."

Warren returned to the sentencing: "Does the record show evidence that the judge heard the information we now have before sentencing?" And he read to the Court Judge Pugh's words as he sentenced John: "Of course the jury didn't believe you; and the jury rightly didn't believe you" through "shall suffer death" and "may God have mercy on your soul."

"How much time elapsed," he asked, "between the trial and the sentencing?"

Needle didn't know. Forer respectfully supplied that it had been six days, and there had been no pre-sentencing investigation.

When the hearing concluded, Needle said, "The State of Maryland will gladly produce for the Court Stella's juvenile record and information on the sentencing."

"Please do," said Warren.

The committee and the lawyers walked out into the sunshine of an October afternoon, and on the sidewalk, reporters closed in on Joe Forer and Frances Ross. (That evening, after her

197

interview on television had been shown, Mrs. Ross received a telephone call which she suspected came from Stella Mae: "Mrs. Ross, your face needs lifting," and the caller hung up.)

A few days later the justices received from the State of Maryland the complete records on Stella from the juvenile courts of both counties. Also, they received from Judge Pugh—the judge who sentenced the Giles—a long affidavit, defending his failure to make a pre-sentencing investigation and his imposing the death sentence. He included what no one had asked for: the police reports of those originally investigating the case. One was two pages long, the other twenty-two. These were the reports Joe Forer had asked again and again to see, only to be refused by Judge Moorman each time.

XX

The Supreme Court could not possibly hand down its decision before January, thought Joe Forer: it would probably come on the ninth. So the prisoners spent from October till January with more peace of mind than they had known in years. And for Joe Forer, the breathing space meant he could work on his other cases without interruption. Harold occupied this unallotted spare time by preparing his family to be amateur radio operators and himself to take the advanced examination.

On Monday, January 9, 1967, Barbara Knapp (primed to race to the basement of the court building to telephone the decision to Harold) and a sprinkling of other committee members stood at the head of the line of tourists waiting to be let into the courtroom to hear the decision, after Warren finished welcoming lawyers to practice before the Court. No decision came. The committee members filed out into the raw January day and the wind which blows hardest on Capitol Hill.

Peace of mind ended at the prison.

John wrote:

> All day I have been catching the news every hour on the hour, hoping for some word from the Court, but so far no such luck . . . . It's almost like someone holding a gun at your head and not knowing if or when they will shoot.

And James wrote:

> Monday passed with me sitting over the radio with my
> heart racing, waiting for the word. Most of yesterday I was
> really depressed that nothing had happened. [The following
> Sunday he wrote:] What I'm mostly thinking about is tomor-
> row. Will it come tomorrow? I am no where near as excited
> now as I was this time last weekend; so if it doesn't come to-
> morrow, then on to the next Monday, or on to the next . . . ."

"On to the next" proved prophetic. For seven Mondays
Barbara fed the children, started them down the road to the
bus stop, and then drove the thirty-odd miles into Washington
to the Supreme Court. Except for Joe Forer and Hal Witt,
she was the only committee member there.

At the penitentiary tension mounted agonizingly. "The
weekends are the worst," said Joe Johnson. "We don't go to
work and we just sit in our cells waiting for Monday."

The decision came on February 20. "We would vacate the
judgment of the Maryland Court of Appeals," said five of the
nine Justices, "and remand to that court for further proceedings."

Barbara ran down the stairs rather than wait for an elevator.

"They've remanded it to the Appeals Court," she told
Harold.

"What does that mean?"

"I don't know and I haven't time to try to think. I want
to get back upstairs and catch Joe."

From the telephone in the basement she headed for the
Clerk's office. The buzzer had just sounded and the opinions
just handed down. She was given two copies and was off
again, this time to the Lawyer's Lounge, meeting Joe Forer
and Hal Witt as they came down the hall. "Joe just looked
dazed," she said. They went into the lounge, looked through
the opinions, and then the two lawyers took off for the penitentiary to explain the decision to the prisoners. "We were so

depressed and angry, and the boys spent all their time trying to cheer us up."

Barbara drove to Harold's office. He shortly took leave for the rest of the day and together they worked at duplicating the opinions, which ran fifty-four pages. At home all that afternoon the phone rang steadily, Gunnar competently noting the messages, after he came home from school. There were calls from friends who had mistaken the decision for a clear victory and wanted to congratulate the Knapps; calls from the Associated Press and from the local and Baltimore presses; calls from radio and television reporters.

Barbara did not reach home till 5:00 and Harold not until almost 7:00. He was too sick at heart, too busy with telephone calls, to run his usual four miles. That night neither of them could sleep. At midnight he got up, put on his clothes for running, started down the drive, slipped on the ice and fell, and returned to the house even more tense than before.

Barbara kept repeating: "It's all because of those police reports. We know Stedman Prescott never read through any twenty-two-page report, and here the Justices think he did."

Joe Forer had warned the committee, in the weeks of waiting, that one possible—and undesirable—outcome would be for the Court to "find some pretext to send the case back to a lower court."

The police reports provided that pretext.

"Thus the case presents," wrote Brennan in the majority opinion,

> the broad questions whether the prosecution's constitutional duty to disclose extends to all evidence admissible and useful to the defense . . . . We find, however, that it is unnecessary, and therefore inappropriate, to examine those questions . . . . We now have evidence before us, which neither Judge Moorman nor the Court of Appeals considered . . . two police

reports, not part of the record, which came to our attention when the State at our request supplied the material considered by the trial judge in imposing sentence . . . .

There can be little doubt that the defense might have made effective use of the report at the trial or in obtaining further evidence. In the first place, the report attributes statements to the girl and Rogers that appear inconsistent with their trial testimony. The report quotes both as stating they were engaged in sexual relations when they were distracted by the noise at Bowie's car, and that the girl dressed before petitioners and Johnson approached. They testified at trial, however, that they were merely "sitting" in the back seat . . . and Rogers buttressed this testimony on cross-examination by answering "No" to the question whether he "didn't take her out there to have sexual relations with her yourself . . . ?" Finally, neither Lieutenant Whelan nor Detective Collins mentioned, in their summaries at trial . . . the fact that the girl and Rogers . . . were engaged in sexual relations when they heard the three men.

The testimony of the girl and Rogers is open to the construction that these key witnesses deliberately concealed from the judge, jury, and defense counsel evidence of the girl's promiscuity . . . .

And how many had had intercourse with Stella Mae that July night? Two or three?

One of the Justices asked Forer during his argument about the point made by the prosecution, that Stella at first had thought emission, not merely penetration, was necessary if the act was to be called rape; and that when her mistake had been explained to her, she corrected her testimony to say all three boys had raped her.

"Oh, sir, that is a mere canard," answered Forer.

The police reports could have been useful on this point as well, Brennan went on, for they quoted Stella's identifying John as "the one who tried to have intercourse with her but was unable to do so . . . yet nothing appears in the trial transcript to show what, if any, action was taken by the prosecution to correct or explain the inconsistencies between the testimony of the State witnesses and the report . . ." although "both Detective Collins and Mr. Kardy who supervised the prosecution had read the report before trial."

Justices White and Harlan assumed Stedman Prescott had read those reports, but Brennan was not sure:

> Since the reports were not produced, it is pure speculation to conclude that trial counsel had in fact seen the reports now before us . . . the Court of Appeals might nevertheless regard an inquiry to be in order to ascertain trial counsel's reasons for not making use of the reports in support of the defense he was directing on behalf of petitioners.
>
> In light of all this . . . in order to avoid deciding constitutional questions by allowing state courts to take action which might dispose of the case . . . We would therefore vacate the judgment of the Court of Appeals and remand to that court for further proceedings.

Justice White wrote a separate opinion, although he went along with the majority. He was puzzled by Judge Moorman's reasoning, when the judge had excluded everything at the post-conviction hearing which had to do with Stella's juvenile record or her mental state. He did not wish to imply that such reasoning was "necessarily incorrect," but he thought such testimony might well have been permitted in evidence.

> In the end, any allegation of suppression boils down to an assessment of what the State knows at trial in comparison to the knowledge held by the defense. It would seem that the Maryland Court of Appeals would reverse as unconstitutional a conviction in a trial that included suppression of evidence . . . concerning the mental condition of the complaining witness and the interrelated issues of her consent and credibility . . . .

But only Abe Fortas met head-on the issue which Joe Forer had hoped the Giles-Johnson case would persuade the Court to resolve; whether a criminal trial was a forensic contest or an effort to arrive at justice. And if the answer was justice, would not the prosecution then have to share with the defense all the evidence which its superior resources for investigation were able to uncover? As Forer had said in his petition to the Supreme Court, there was a "grass roots" movement toward that end. Almost every reputable law journal or quarterly had recently carried at least one article pleading for "discovery" or "disclosure" by the prosecution. Ten years before, California had adopted a liberal rule; Illinois had just done so.

> Yet many states, while responding in some degree to this trend, have been slow to revise the traditional, restrictive approach which, it is submitted, hinders the criminal of little means in the preparation of his defense and makes a mockery of the constitutional guarantees demanded by an enlightened system of criminal justice.*

(A few years before, Justice Brennan himself had titled a speech, "The Criminal Prosecution: Sporting Event or Quest for Truth?")

Justice Fortas began his brief opinion:

> I concur in the Court's judgment in this immensely troubling case, but I do so for the reasons which led the Montgomery County Circuit Court to order a new trial . . . that the prosecution was under a duty to disclose, and that its omission to do so required a new trial . . . .
>
> I do not agree that the State may be excused from its duty to disclose material facts known to it prior to trial . . . the State's obligation is not to convict, but to see that, so far as possible, truth emerges. This is also the ultimate statement of its responsibility to provide a fair trial under the Due Process Clause of the Fourteenth Amendment . . . .
>
> The story of the prosecutrix is a tragic one. But our total

* Draft Statute, *"A State Statute to Liberalize Criminal Discovery,"* 4 Harv. J. Legis. 107 (1966).

lack of sympathy for the kind of physical assault which is involved here may not lead us to condone state suppression of information which might be useful to the defense . . . . I would vacate the judgment of conviction and require the case to be retried. In view of the conclusions of the majority, however, I concur . . . in sending this case back to the Court of Appeals for reconsideration.

Justice Harlan, called "the Court's most convinced believer in the value of state independence," was controlled by that belief in his decision. He wrote the dissent, joined by Black, Clark, and Stewart.

> The disposition of this case . . . is wholly out of keeping with the constitutional limitations upon this Court's role in the review of state criminal cases . . . .
>
> On the basis of the trial record, it would be difficult to imagine charges more convincingly proved than were those against the three youths for raping this teenage girl . . . .
>
> [The] police reports . . . played a significant role throughout the state court proceedings . . . . There is no basis whatever in the evidence before us for the plurality's intimation that the reports seen by counsel may not have been those given to the Court or for its thinly veiled suggestion that in not making use of the report counsel may have been incompetent or worse.
>
> . . . Under defense counsel's persistent cross-examination she [Stella] repeatedly affirmed that she was telling the full truth, and that she did not know "what I thought" at the time of her earlier accounts. Given her age and circumstances, this is scarcely improbable . . . . [Footnote]
>
> Neither [police] report was intended to serve as a formal and precise record; it is therefore extraordinarily hazardous to pyramid, as the plurality has done, hypotheses upon strained constructions of the reports' most abbreviated references . . . .
>
> Perhaps more evidence of Stella's mental condition, and of the knowledge of Montgomery County authorities of that condition, could conceivably have been introduced; but it is true

of all criminal prosecutions, federal and state, that some fragments of fact broadly pertinent to the issues of the trial do not reach the record.

He could not subscribe to

my Brother Fortas's approach [which] would demand markedly broader disclosures than this Court has ever held the Fourteenth Amendment to require . . . . [They] would entirely alter the character and balance of our present systems of criminal justice . . . . We on this bench are not free to disturb a state conviction simply for reasons that might be permissible were we sitting on the state court of last resort. Nor are we free to interject our individual sympathies into the administration of state criminal justice.

Of his opinion Fortas wrote in his Addendum:

My Brother Harlan has addressed a section of his dissent to my concurring opinion. This discloses a basic difference between us with respect to the State's responsibility under the fair trial requirement of the Fourteenth Amendment. I believe that deliberate concealment and nondisclosure by the State are not to be distinguished in principle from misrepresentation . . . . Mr. Justice Harlan concedes that the State may not knowingly use perjured testimony or allow it to remain uncorrected. He asserts that this satisfies "in full" the requirements of the Fourteenth Amendment, and an "extension of these principles is . . . neither necessary nor advisable." . . . I assume that Mr. Justice Harlan would apply this principle, even though the information might, in the hands of defense counsel, spell the difference between death and the exoneration of the defendant.

I cannot subscribe to this. A criminal trial is not a game in which the State's function is to outwit and entrap its quarry. The State's pursuit is justice, not a victim . . . .

"A murder trial—" he wrote, echoing the title of Justice Brennan's speech, "indeed any criminal proceeding—is not a sporting event."

"Well, we didn't lose, but we didn't win," said Joe Forer, trying to explain to the committee the Supreme Court decision, which, he reiterated, really was not a decision. "But I will say this much: I think that very inability of the Justices to decide this case indicates that the committee has made a dent on the public conscience. You've read the opinions . . . how Fortas said this was a 'disturbing case,' and Harlan says the Court is 'uneasy with the convictions.' Now what did they mean? The Court gets cases every day of terrible injustice which they don't attempt to review on the valid grounds that they can't correct all the injustices. No, it was something more than that: it was disturbing because it was an injustice the public had picked up.

"That recent editorial in the *Post* expresses that—how the public has picked up the feeling that there's something very wrong here—and inasmuch as the committee has shown there was something wrong, we've made some difference in the legal system. The *Post* was saying, 'You ought to do something about this.' They didn't say about this particular case— maybe they want the Giles and Joe Johnson to be martyrs; they want them to be the occasion to reform the legal system.

"But Fortas also called it an 'immensely disturbing case' because it looked as though the people were innocent and yet the Constitutional doctrines are not adequate to let people out merely because they're innocent. Innocence is a relatively irrelevant factor of American law."

XXI

"The Giles case keeps leaking new evidence," editorialized the *Washington Post* (February 23, 1967).

> It has been through five and a half years of trials, hearings and appeals. Yet at each stage, new facts emerge. The trial juries, it now is clear, heard only a fragment of the story. More facts came out in the Governor's Clemency hearing. Still more came out in the hearing on suppression of evidence. Now, most astonishing of all, new facts emerge from the appeal to the Supreme Court of the United States. The most disquieting aspect of this case is the clear showing that even after five and a half years, no court has heard all of the relevant and admissible evidence.

Once the Supreme Court had seen the police reports and put them into evidence, Joe Forer was free to act on his original suspicion—one shared by Justice Brennan—that Stedman Prescott, the Giles' lawyer in 1961, had never seen all of those reports. Quite right, said Prescott. When he was shown Kardy's file, he said, he did not see either the twenty-two-page "B" or the shorter "C" report. In his affidavit on the subject, he wrote, in part:

> 5. The police report which I did see prior to the trial did not contain any information that Stella Mae Watkins and William Rogers had been having intercourse in the car the night they had their encounter with the Giles brothers and Joseph Johnson. Nor did I have any information from any

other source to that effect. The police report which I saw prior to the trial did not contain any information that Stella Mae Watkins had stated to the police that only two men had entered her.

6. In my opinion it would have been most useful to me in defending the Giles brothers if I had seen, prior to their trial, the police reports attached to Judge Pugh's affidavit . . . .

Prescott signed his affidavit on February 28. On March 15, Kardy countered with his own, saying he had shared his file, including report "C," with Prescott. And as to report "B," "I personally read the matters and things contained therein to Mr. Stedman Prescott, Jr., as they applied to his clients . . ." ("Twenty-two pages are a lot to read aloud," commented Joe Forer.)

Forer included both affidavits at the end of his brief for the Maryland Court of Appeals. It was a printed booklet of twenty-five closely reasoned and annotated pages which had to do with the discrepancies between what Stella Mae, William Rogers, and the three police officers had said on the witness stand and what they had said originally in the police reports. He submitted the brief on March 28 and argued the matter a few days later in the same small, elegantly formal room in Annapolis, with its red carpeting and red velvet curtains. As had happened two years before, the committee, sponsors, and friends were too many for the accommodations, and in spite of the chairs which were brought in, several had to sit on the radiators or stand at one side.

In its decision announced within a week, the Appeals Court made no mention whatsoever of either affidavit, or of the examples of "false testimony" Forer had brought out in his brief. Having the Giles case dropped in its hands for the fourth time, it swiftly reviewed it and, following the example of the Supreme Court, remanded it to a lower court. They were remanding it, they said pointedly, not because they conceded anything as to the legality of the "issues" raised by Forer and Witt, but because "there exist questions which cannot at this time be adequately resolved without the aid of further Evidentiary Proceedings." They instructed the Montgomery County Circuit Court to handle it as a continuation of the post-conviction hearing of 1964.

That the Appeals Court would remand was almost a foregone conclusion. In the two years since it had reversed Moorman's order for a new trial, one of the judges voting then with the majority had been replaced and one of the two then dissenting was now the chief judge. Other factors contributed: the flamboyant Leonard Kardy, who "had never asked the death sentence" but had persuaded the juries in both the Giles case and the Johnson case to impose it, had dropped out of public life. He had given up his plan to run for Congress and, retiring to private practice, had made no effort to run again as State's Attorney for Montgomery County.

His successor was William Linthicum, who had "respectfully" urged the Appeals Court to remand the case to the lower court. (The Attorney General of Maryland also urged the same.) Almost all the committee had worked for Linthicum's election. He was thirty-six, black-haired, brown-eyed, and wore glasses; open-faced, eager, and earnest, he had a habit of pursing his lips frequently. He was an Ivy-League type who had gone to a correct preparatory school in Washington, was awarded Phi Beta Kappa at Haverford, and took his law degree at Georgetown University. He had been active in all progressive movements in the county, and in its early days had even made a contribution to the Giles-Johnson Defense Committee.

The reopened post-conviction hearing was set for mid-May. Even before that time Forer decided to see whether the case might not leak still some more evidence: would it be possible to see the original Grand Jury records? An anonymous tip, by telephone, to Harold Knapp suggested that Stella's testimony before them and at the trial had varied. Only another expensive, time-consuming litigious action would reveal whether or not the tip was correct—and only, of course, if the judge hearing Forer's arguments was persuaded to produce records which were traditionally secret and not to be seen except in "proven emergencies."

The hearing on the motion was held late in April in a small, relatively intimate Rockville courtroom. The spectators by now had an intimacy of their own, like an extended family; Jackie Giles Bishop (this time without her small son); Sandra Giles Johnson (her husband was one of Joe Johnson's brothers), red hair now cut short; great-uncle Caleb Adams; Edith Throckmorton, head of the Montgomery County NAACP; the executive committee, filling a row in the small center section. It now held a new member, Sam Legge of Baltimore, an educator and Quaker whom Marie Ferington (also a Quaker) had interested in the case. On the left, out in force, was the press, most of whom the committee knew so well that they, too, seemed part of the extended family.

The Giles brothers sat in a reserved section, at right angles to both the judge and the spectators: John in gray trousers, dark jacket, white shirt open at the throat, no tie; James, with tie and black suit. When they came in everyone smiled or waved to them, and John was finally relaxed enough with the committee to smile back.

To complete the illusion of family, there at the front and presiding was Judge Moorman, who had heard the first post-conviction argument three summers before, and who had been the only judge—so far—to forthrightly order a new trial. Not noticeably grayer than he had been, but heavier.

Linthicum did not seriously oppose Forer's motion to see the records, but what really concerned Judge Moorman, it transpired, was whether the Court had the power to "disclose" the contents to the defense: he had found no precedent in

Maryland law. Forer countered that since the case had been thrown back into the post-conviction stage, Moorman's decision would be such as might be made in a civil case, where "disclosure" or "discovery" were permissible. Forer added that he had hoped the Supreme Court would use the Giles case as a basis for ruling that "discovery" was vital in criminal cases as well.

"You will have to clarify that Supreme Court decision for me sometime, Mr. Forer," said Judge Moorman.

"I would be glad to. I agree it needs explaining. In fact, with all due respect to the august bodies who have ruled on this case, we have found your decision the best, Your Honor."

The extended family burst into laughter and Judge Moorman—although he did not permit himself to laugh—turned his head to one side, his face flushed with pleasure.

"I don't get that every day," he said.

The hearing was brief. As always the Giles were led out the instant the door closed behind the judge. The committee pursued them—knowing its way around the courthouse from experience—to the basement, past the sheriff's office, and out into the back courtyard, where they found they had been anticipated by TV and press photographers. At length the guards brought the Giles up the steps from the lower basement, shoved them into a car, and they were off.

Moorman had said he would reach a quick decision, and he did. His six-page opinion, agreeing to let the defense see the records, said in part,

> When the reasons for clothing grand jury testimony in secrecy have disappeared, the cloak should be lifted . . . . Reasons for preserving secrecy are non-existent in this case . . . . It is patently clear that parts of . . . two police reports are inconsistent with testimony given by the two grand jury witnesses (Stella Mae and William Rogers) at trial.

In the three weeks remaining before the post-conviction hearing on May 15—also before Judge Moorman—the pace of the Knapp household became almost as frantic as it had been before the original hearing. The telephone rang at all hours; Harold lunched almost daily with Joe Forer; and both Knapps met with Forer and Witt, night after night, to plan. ("They all three fell asleep one night," said Barbara.) And though no Blue Report was being prepared, Harold's letter-writing to try to find witnesses occupied almost as much time.

A Richard Johnson proved to be the most elusive. Some years before he had called Frances Ross to say he had information about Stella Mae which the committee might find useful, but had then failed to keep an appointment with Forer and Harold Knapp and was forgotten. Harold remembered him now, only to learn that he had left the area, and no one in the apartment building where he had lived most recently knew where he was.

So, like other hapless "possible witnesses" before him, Richard Johnson became the "one missing piece in a thousand-word puzzle" which—according to Dotty Brooks—Harold would not stop until he found. He resorted to old telephone books, previous addresses, and went to one apartment building after another, knocking on doors on each floor, to ask the tenant within whether he had ever known a former tenant named Richard Johnson. The answer was so consistently "No" that he was almost ready to give up when he discovered a woman who had not known Richard, but had known his mother, a Mrs. Olson, and produced an address for her in the West. Harold and Joe Forer composed a letter to Mrs. Olson, explaining why they wanted to get in touch with her son. It was carefully worded. All too often Harold had found mothers wanting to protect their children from any publicity, and suspected Mrs. Olson would be similarly uncooperative.

On the contrary: she not only supplied her son's address, but wrote that it was she, in the first place, who had suggested that Richard call the committee. Letters and telephone calls shuttled back and forth, with the result that the committee arranged to fly both Mrs. Olson and her son to Washington to take the stand as witnesses at the post-conviction hearing on May 15.

The two arrived late on the preceding Saturday afternoon. Mrs. Olson was quiet, modest, and well-spoken, her fair hair now graying. Richard, twenty-six, was also fair, but with red hair. The Knapps met them and took them home with them and on Sunday afternoon, in the Knapps' light-filled living room, Mrs. Olson dictated her affidavit. Later, Richard—not wishing to talk in front of his mother—dictated his to Harold and Joe Forer in the playroom on the lower floor, but it added little to his mother's except more evidence of Stella Mae's promiscuity. ("But she did not seem to either enjoy or not enjoy these relations; it was all a mechanical thing with her.")

His mother's was less lengthy, but more specific. After the first paragraph of identification, it read:

> 2. One afternoon in September, 1962, when I returned home from work, my son Richard told me he had spoken by phone to a girl he knew named Stella Mae Watkins and she had told him to look on page 3 of the *Washington Post* because she was all over it. He said that he had looked but that he couldn't find her name. I then looked at the paper and also could not find Stella Watkins' name mentioned on page 3.
>
> 3. I have been shown a photocopy of page 3 of the *Washington Post* for September 26, 1962, attached hereto and marked Exhibit A. I am quite sure that that is the page we looked at.
>
> 4. Richard told me that the girl was going to call him back soon and that I could listen in if I wished.

5. Soon after that the phone rang. I answered it in the kitchen. A girl's voice asked for Richard. Richard went upstairs to take the call and I stayed on the kitchen phone.

6. Richard told her he hadn't found her name on the page, and she asked if he had read the story about the rape case, and said that she was the girl in the case. Richard asked her if that had really happened to her.

7. I believe I can quote her answer almost in the exact words she used. She said: "Those boys are telling the truth. I offered it to them. I always heard that a Nigger was bigger and better than a white man, and I wanted to know if it was the truth."

8. I was disgusted and hung up the phone.

9. The next day at my office in Washington, D.C., during my lunch period which was sometime between 12:30 and 2:00 P.M., I started to read the day's *Washington Daily News*. I saw an article there about the same rape case which had been the subject of the *Washington Post* story I had seen the day before. I have been shown a photocopy of page 5 of the *Washington Daily News* of September 27, 1962, attached hereto as Exhibit B. I am sure that the article by Samuel Stafford which appears there is the one I saw.

10. The article gave the name of the State's Attorney and referred to the Giles brothers.

11. I obtained from telephone information the telephone number for the Montgomery County State's Attorney's Office. I dialed the number. I believe that the operator came on the line, thus indicating that it was then an interzone call, and put the call through. A feminine voice answered "State's Attorney's Office." I asked to speak to Mr. Kardy, the State's Attorney. The woman who answered asked my name. I told her my name, and said that Mr. Kardy wouldn't know me, but I was calling in reference to the Giles brothers case. She told me Mr. Kardy was on another line, and I agreed to wait.

12. Then a man's voice said "Hello." I asked "Is this Mr. Kardy, the State's Attorney?" He said "Yes." I stated my name and that I was calling in reference to the girl in

215

the Giles brothers case. I asked if her name was Stella, then paused, and he said "Yes.' I then said "Mae," and he said "Yes, Watkins."

13. I told him that the girl had called my son the preceding night and repeated to him what I had heard her say to Richard on the telephone. Mr. Kardy answered, "We have all the evidence we need." The case had already gone to the jury and there was nothing that could be done about it.

Monday morning was cool, as the whole spring had been, but the sun held promise. The Knapps, with Richard and his mother (almost ill with nervousness at the ordeal ahead), arrived early to sit in the center section, front row, of big, familiar Courtroom #1 in Rockville, where Judge Moorman had rebuked Harold Knapp for selling the Blue Report in 1964. It filled rapidly. Committee members inured to this routine had supplied themselves with Life Savers to take the edge off the mounting hunger of the long hours, and some, who had frequently sat on those hard, pew-like benches, brought cushions. Recognizing this as the beginning of a climactic session, many of the sponsors had come as well.

Joe Forer and Hal Witt sat at their table with the Giles beside them; William Linthicum and his assistant Andrew Sonner sat at theirs with a man several people in the room recognized as the Attorney General of the State of Maryland, Francis Burch.

Linthicum began. The State had conducted, with the cooperation of the Attorney General, a full investigation of the matter before the court. That investigation, he told Moorman, had caused the State to reevaluate its position, since the information produced indicated that the records of the Montgomery County police—agents of the State—were open to serious question. On requesting all the police reports, his office had been given not only the typed ones, but also the original handwritten notes which an officer had jotted down when he interviewed Stella after the episode on Batson Road.

He had himself, Linthicum went on, studied those handwritten notes: Stella's words, which stood out among the hastily scribbled sentences, were "The third c/m did not have intercourse; he only kissed me a couple of times." But on the witness stand, the same officer who had scribbled those words quoted Stella as saying three men had assaulted her. (Also in those notes, not mentioned by Linthicum, were comments made by Stella Mae which might have had relevance to later identifications in the line-ups: "I can identify the bigger one of the 3 c/m but I am not sure about the other two. It was dark and I could not see their faces very well.")

"Are you saying," Judge Moorman asked Linthicum, "that the State confesses error in that there was perjured testimony?"

"The State confesses error," said Linthicum in a heavy tone. Then he paused. "But I would rather not characterize the testimony of the officers. That's before the Grand Jury. We would respectfully request the Court for a new trial." He sat down.

Attorney General Burch then rose to address the bench. Not only did he concur in the request for a new trial, but he felt impelled to express his admiration for the State's Attorney of Montgomery County, Linthicum, for being "more interested in seeing that justice was done, than in sustaining a conviction in this case."

Joe Forer's turn was next. He, too, wished to commend Linthicum for personally studying the notes which implicated the police; of course he concurred in the request for a new trial. He said a few more words, after which Linthicum rose again. He wished to add, he said, that there was "nothing to indicate improper conduct on the part of the former State's Attorney for Montgomery County [Kardy] or his staff."

The ultimate act was Moorman's. Hand across forehead, he sat with bowed head for what seemed to the spectators, who sat in hushed silence, to be several minutes. Then he removed the hand and lifted his head.

"John and James Giles, stand up," he said to the startled brothers (James had been busy taking notes). "I presume your counsel has explained to you that in the event of a new trial and a possible conviction, you could be sentenced to death?"

"We fully understand," answered James.

"The Court takes judicial notice of the nature of the evidence in the form of police reports. The Court is of the opinion that these defendants have been deprived of their liberty without due process of law. The conviction against them is set aside . . . they will remain in the custody of the institution where they are presently confined until further order of this Court. You may sit down."

The Giles sat down.

"The Court," continued Moorman, "would feel derelict in its duty if it failed to commend the State's Attorney for his conduct in laying bare the reasons for which this court has granted a new trial. It is too bad that a forthright presentation of that error has not been made in the past."

He stood up; the audience rose and watched him leave the bench. Once again the Giles were out of the room almost as quickly as the judge.

The spectators that morning were beyond control. They stood talking in the courtroom until the sheriff evicted them; then they stood in the corridor outside until a guard approached: "Y'all really *must* leave this corridor." They moved out to the back courtyard in time to wave the Giles off in the car returning them to the penitentiary; then they returned to the front of the courthouse, reluctant to leave each other. One after another, various members of the family and the committee were interrogated and photographed.

"You've grown very artful over the years," said one interviewer to Frances Ross as she parried his questions.

"The whole affair," reported the *Sentinel* in its next issue (May 18, 1967), "accomplished in 15 minutes what a Montgomery County Group called the Giles-Johnson Defense Committee has been trying to accomplish for 5 years, but it would not have happened without the committee."

At its next executive meeting, the committee learned that what they came to call "The Day the State Confessed Error" had been carefully rehearsed, almost choreographed. On the preceding Wednesday, Forer had had a call to come at once to Annapolis. He picked up Hal Witt and went. In the Attorney General's office, Linthicum explained to them about the notes he had read, and about which he had just been talking to Attorney General Burch. The State, he explained, planned to confess error and ask for a new trial. The defense lawyers were pledged to secrecy ("that's why we had to bring Mrs. Olson and Richard east anyway") and also to promising that they would make no dramatic speeches.

"They were afraid we would want our high moment of triumph in court," said Forer. "So then we all went to talk to Judge Moorman, to provide him *his* moment of drama, and also to let him know he wouldn't be sitting on our case for three days or a week.

"The only one who forgot his lines," Forer continued, "was Linthicum. He was blushing so hard in embarrassment over quoting Stella's alley-level words to the police about her experience that he forgot his plan to exonerate Kardy. So when I made my small speech of commendation I gave him his clue. That's why he rose again to say there was 'nothing to indicate any improper conduct on the part of the former State's Attorney.' "

XXII

A half hour after he had accepted the tributes of the bench
and those standing before it that dramatic day ("Should be
commended. . . ." "Highest traditions of a State's Attorney. . . ."
"More interested in seeing justice done than in sustaining a
conviction . . . ."), William Linthicum was meeting with the
Grand Jury, summoned to decide whether the two police officers had been guilty of "any criminal action as a result of
questionable testimony."

The Grand Jury decided that they had not, to the bewilder-
ment of the committee, which thought juries decided on the
basis of facts. Had not the State confessed that morning that
they had given false testimony?

"Prosecutors," said Forer, "can usually get a Grand Jury to
go along with what they want."

"I served on a Grand Jury once," added Lew Maddocks, vice-
chairman of the committee, "back in Ohio. And I noticed that
every time the prosecutor made it clear he thought he had a
good case, the Grand Jury indicted; when he was uncertain
whether he could convict, the jury didn't indict. It only took
a majority, either way: it wasn't like a petty jury."

The failure to indict the two policemen gave the committee
its first clue that Linthicum was as politically-minded as the
public usually assumed all prosecuting attorneys were. The
second clue came when Joe Forer tried to get the Giles brothers

out on bail. He thought Linthicum had agreed not to oppose bail, but when the court session was held Linthicum not only opposed bail but said he would present the case as soon as possible before a legally constituted Grand Jury for a fresh indictment. "I have every confidence that given that indictment, I can succeed in getting them reconvicted."

He acted promptly. Stella Mae was located in Florida, having been divorced and remarried, but by the time the detective dispatched to produce her arrived in Florida, she had taken her two children (one by the first husband) and disappeared. Linthicum proceeded without her, using William Rogers as witness and supplying the Grand Jury with the transcript of the original trial.* (Forer and Witt asked to be called as witnesses in order to present evidence new since the transcript; they were refused.) The Grand Jury reindicted the brothers not only on the count of rape, but also on those—previously thrown out—of assault and battery and of robbery. (The robbery referred to the quarter James had accepted from William.)

The committee met the next night, a hot one in June. Joe Forer sat in his usual place before the fireplace, sport shirt open at the throat, and spoke with more anger in his voice than the committee had ever heard before.

"I want a release for the press as soon as possible. All along we've been too nice, too polite; this time we must say what we really think."

But it was long before the members could put their minds to saying on paper what they really thought. They were too much preoccupied with the seeming contradictions they found in Linthicum: how had someone for whom so many of them

* "The prosecutor need present only enough evidence to satisfy statutory requirements for bringing of indictments," according to the Minnesota Annotated Statutes, for example. "The Grand Jury shall find an indictment when all the evidence, taken together, is such as in its judgment would—if unexplained and uncontradicted—warrant a conviction by a trial jury."

had voted, whom they had respected, who had been active in every progressive movement in the county—how had he come to belie everything for which he had once appeared to stand?

"And he comes from such a fine old Maryland family," someone quoted.

"We all come from old families," said Forer.

"Linthicum's the nicest man I've ever been the maddest at," said Harold Knapp.

"Well, I can see he's in a bad spot," said Barbara. "Not that that excuses him. But when we went to see him he told us that he'd had so much hate mail since the day he confessed the State's error, and the police in the county are furious and think he let them down."

"How can they think that?" came from another side of the room. "All along he's been protecting them; look how he got the Grand Jury *not* to indict the two policemen who had committed perjury; look how he's been protecting Kardy, how he exonerated him that day the State confessed. Look how he's been trying to make everybody happy—except, of course, the Giles brothers. What he wants is to come out of it all as the great mediator."

"There's no one more dangerous," said Forer, "than a man convinced he's acting from a sense of rectitude."

The statement for the press, which they finally drafted, was six paragraphs long, some harsher than others; it ended with "We ask that the indictments against the Giles brothers be dismissed."

3. This case has been marked by inadequate police investigation, suppression of evidence, use of false testimony, and the imposition of savage sentences. We cannot but conclude that the case is a tragic instance of a double standard of justice, and that the situation would have been very different had the defendants been middle or upper class white youths.

4. The same Grand Jury which reindicted the Giles brothers in a perfunctory session, refused to indict any police witness despite prima facie evidence of perjury at the trial.
5. We are shocked that the State has reindicted them not only on the rape charge, but also on charges previously abandoned by the State, that they robbed the girl's escort of $.25.
6. In view of the circumstances of this case, no one can have any confidence in the reliability of the evidence which the State may produce at a retrial in which the lives of the Giles brothers will be at stake.

Linthicum had asked to have the Giles trial and any litigation connected with it transferred to another county, on the grounds that there had been too much publicity in the Washington area. The county picked was Towson, a suburb of Baltimore; the date for the trial was the following October.

Now, with a different circuit court involved, Forer again asked for the Giles to be released on bond, and on July 5, the "concerned citizens," as the newspapers frequently called the committee, left home early for the drive to Towson.

There they found themselves in a small, old-fashioned courtroom, with two tiers of benches rising abruptly to the ceiling, and the walnut paneling and rails polished over so many years that they were now a gleaming black. The committee saw, with a sigh of relief, that Mr. Giles was sitting with his daughters and relatives. They knew he had sold the family home, bought a small farm in another county, and ever since his wife's death had had no contact with his sons, being unable to forgive them for her death, which he felt their conduct had precipitated. His presence now meant reconciliation.

Aunt Elsie was also there, Mrs. Giles's sister. She lived in Baltimore, the wife of a merchant seaman presently at sea and the mother of nine. She was abundantly fat, genial, full of bounce and spirit. "If the boys get let out," she said, striking her breast, "they're coming right home to Mama."

Judge John G. Turnbull, who would decide whether the Giles went home or back to the penitentiary, had red cheeks, black hair parted in the middle and plastered to his head, and an air of "no nonsense."

"I will try to give a capsule history of this case," began Joe Forer.

"How could anybody do that?" asked Turnbull, and continued to thwart any attempt on Forer's part to recapitulate. The only question before the court, Turnbull insisted, was whether or not there should be bail for the Giles. What were the precedents? One of Linthicum's assistants said they were to the effect of no bail in capital cases. But then—would he really come through, this time?—Linthicum rose and said, "We do not oppose bail."

"How much bail had you considered?" Turnbull asked Forer, and at long last the spectators dared to smile at each other, as did John to James, sitting at the table below them. Turnbull usually did not grant bail in capital cases, he said, but "the court cannot close its eyes to the extensive incarceration of these defendants. They would have been paroled if they had received an eight-year sentence for second-degree murder, for example. However . . . ." But his "however" had only to do with the amount of bail, $10,000 seeming to him a more fitting amount than the lower figure Forer had suggested.

James executed a little dance step as the sheriff led the two brothers out the door behind the bench.

Out in the corridor, jubilation took over, interrupted only by the practical matter of the actual release: Marie Ferington handed Joe Forer the money that the committee had decided the Giles would need to start a new life; the Carl Hershes—a quiet, middle-aged couple always interested in the case, but not on the executive committee—waited with the deed of their house as bond for one brother; the Knapps with the deed of theirs for the other. Led by Forer and Witt and trailed by the press, the two couples went to the basement room where the formalities would take place. The process took more than an hour, for the Giles's signatures were needed and an official had to go to the penitentiary in the old center of Baltimore to obtain them. Finally the Knapps, the Giles family, the lawyers, Sam Legge, and the press all made their way to the penitentiary.

In the sunshine of that July noon, the gray fortress looked less grim. The group gathered in its entryway, at the head of the stone steps with their spiked balustrades, outside the first of the series of grilled doorways. Mr. Giles sat on one of the benches beside Aunt Elsie, miserably answering "Fine, just fine" to the "How do you feel?" which one reporter after another asked him. "What are you going to give them to eat?" another asked Aunt Elsie. She answered with gusto: "Fried chicken, collard greens, the best cornbread they ever ate." Then she called across the entryway to Jackie: "Jacqueline, what do you think your brothers would like for dessert?" Sweet potato pudding was agreed upon and Aunt Elsie furnished the recipe for the reporter, who was a woman.

"Don't tell the press where you live," Sam Legge said to Aunt Elsie; "if they find out you'll have no peace."

Before long the street at the foot of the steps became almost impassable, cluttered with TV and radio trucks and with press cars. In the entryway the waiting dragged on and on; on the inside officials came and went; a guard once unlocked the doors to admit Jackie and her little boy to the toilet, and once again to permit the Knapps to unload their seven-year file of the *New Yorker* magazine for the prison library; Joe Forer and Hal Witt were admitted to see Joe Johnson. Still no Giles. An hour and a half had passed and it was getting on toward 2:30.

At last the farthest grilled doors on the inside were opened and some corrugated boxes were shoved through; then very distantly, it seemed, two dark-suited figures appeared. Across the street a *Washington Post* photographer jumped onto the top of a car, adjusting his telescopic lens; within the covered entryway a photographer for a local paper balanced himself and his cameras on the back of a bench; still another climbed on top of the mailbox.

"Here come our celebrities," muttered the guard as he swung open the front doors to let the Giles and their boxes through. (John did not surrender a shoe box to family or friends who were helping carry the heavy ones. It held his pet turtle. The books they had collected, their friends learned later, they had taken around to the inmates of Death Row.)

For a full half hour the press interviewed and photographed them in their ill-fitting prison-made suits, until at last they were released from the ordeal to get into the waiting cars and be driven not—as the press had expected—to Aunt Elsie's, but circuitously to Sam Legge's house, where his wife had a cold lunch waiting. It was a gay occasion for all except John and James, who sat quietly, trying to talk but not succeeding, and clearly in a state of shock. Seeing this, Joe Forer took over and with quip after quip managed to relax them. A call was put through to Frances Ross, at a ranch in Wyoming where she and her husband were bird-watching, and both brothers talked to her. Then, at four o'clock, the cars turned back into the center of Baltimore, heading for the old section just three blocks from the penitentiary. There the brothers, the turtle, and the boxes were deposited in Aunt Elsie's three-story row house to begin living in the outside world, including sweet potato pudding.

In the four months before the trial, John continued to live with his aunt, doing garden and landscaping jobs. James moved to an uncle's in Prince George's County and held a part-time clerical job in the office of the Christian Social Action Council of the United Churches of Christ, where Lew Maddocks was the Council's liaison with Congress. "It's like a course in political science," said James. "They put out a report every week and sometimes they let me write some of it."

Harold Knapp worked on collecting affidavits, trying to trace this or that one of the original cast of characters surrounding Stella Mae and William. It was more difficult than it had been the first time. The intervening years had obscured their trails, but Harold redoubled his efforts and succeeded in supplying several potential witnesses whom Forer could subpoena to be deposed. But no matter how many Harold flushed up, he was not content, affidavits having become almost an obsession with him at this stage.

"Would it help if I got more affidavits?" he asked at one meeting.

"No!" said Forer. "Harold, you not only don't see the forest for the trees, but you don't see the trees for the twigs."

Harold grinned.

"I yield to your implied criticism."

He had now reversed roles and found himself, to his astonishment, a source of information for the police. Police in a New Jersey town where William Rogers had once worked— and where Harold's long-ago inquiries were evidently still on file—asked if he could supply the address of William, wanted on a desertion and non-support charge. On a chance, Harold called the Laurel police and learned that they not only had a local address for William, but that he had been arrested for "disorderly conduct" for fighting (and let go after he had posted collateral); that his permit to drive had been revoked; and that he had also been arrested not long before because he did "make an assault, . . . did beat, bruise, wound and ill-treat one Annabelle Peterson."

The Knapps felt hopeful about this, and longed to have William in jail at the time of the trial. But their hopes were unfulfilled. When his trial for assault came up in September in a little People's Courtroom, it could not have been more

227

perfunctory. The golden-haired woman, divorced mother of five and a waitress in a Laurel inn, said that William had tried to rape her; she had resisted; he had beaten her up and she had succeeded in getting away. She had gone to the police the next day. (No policeman was called to testify.) William—with a slight potbelly now—testified that he had been drinking excessively, had passed out, and hence had not touched her. Why had he picked her up and taken her to that apartment in the first place? "To make love," said William. The judge looked from one to the other with disgust. "A most distasteful case: a mother of five children picking up a man; a married man and a father, admitting planning to commit adultery. Very unsavory. Not guilty."

William's capers continued almost up to the trial, and Harold continued to find out about them, his informant now being William's wife. ("I'll really miss that guy when this is all over," said Harold. "He always acts so predictably.") On September 22, William had not come home until 6:00 in the morning. Finding his wife angry and recriminating, he beat her up and departed, going south—as was later learned—with another woman. (Her husband trailed the two and one of the woman's children, discovered all three in bed together, was "assaulted" by William, and had him arrested. As was usual with William Rogers, he was not jailed but merely "put on probation" in the North Carolina town where the episode had taken place. He was last known to be "heading west," and the woman returned to her husband.)

So William Rogers was not in the courtroom in Towson on October 30, when the Giles came to trial for the second time. Nor, indeed, was the other key witness, Stella Mae (although unknown to many, her mother—hair now auburn—sat in one of the back rows). The "extended family" was there, however, well ahead of the scheduled 10:00 A.M. trial: Aunt Elsie— "I haven't been able to sleep a wink all last week"; John and

James, handsome in new, dark suits, had not slept too well themselves, but they had been staying with the Knapps, at least separated from Aunt Elsie's infectious apprehension; sister Jackie, her husband, and their four-year-old son; the uncles; the committee and the usual members of the press.

Circuit Judge W. Albert Menchine was short-nosed, gray-moustached and undistinguished looking. But to some who had come to hear Forer argue a minor phase of the case before him a few weeks earlier, he had seemed to listen and evaluate Forer's arguments on an exclusively intellectual level, as few other judges before him in the long history of the case had done, and they felt hopeful. His first move was to dispatch the waiting jurors to another room to be on call. Then Linthicum rose.

He wished respectfully to submit the transcript of the 1961 trial. Later he would request its consideration in lieu of testimony by the two accusers; in the meantime, he wished to offer proof that efforts had been made to find and produce the key witnesses.

"I call Detective Sergeant John Kennedy," he said, and Kennedy, a mild-mannered man in his late thirties, swore to tell nothing but the truth and sat down in the witness box. The truth, it appeared, was that efforts to have Stella Mae extradited from Florida had proved useless. A hearing had been held in a Florida court. Stella, eight months pregnant with her second child by this marriage, was explicit in her refusal to go through again, on a witness stand, the events of that night on Batson Road. If forced to appear on the witness stand in Maryland, she said, she would take the oath and sit in the box, but refuse to utter a single word. The Florida court did not order her extradited.

"Now, Detective Kennedy," said Linthicum, "please tell the Court what efforts you made to get William Rogers to testify today."

"Well, last Wednesday I went to Laurel with the summons and his wife said he'd left home on the twenty-second and she'd not seen him since."

Detective Kennedy had not let it go at that. He had called William's mother and learned that William, lacking money, had called her the night before. Should he call again, would his mother please ask him to call Detective Kennedy collect. So he did, and Kennedy had set up a four-way long-distance telephone conversation between the two of them, Linthicum, and his assistant.

"Why hadn't the State seen fit to send him the money to bring him back for the trial, since he seemed willing to be a witness?" The question was Forer's.

"Because," said Kennedy, shifting a little in his chair, "I advised against sending it."

"Why?"

"Because of the unreliability of the witness."

The extended family burst into united, gleeful laughter.

Judge Menchine's face became almost purple with anger.

"Another such outburst in this court and those guilty of it will be sent to jail. I repeat, to jail."

"I mean, unreliable as to time and place," Kennedy added as soon as he could be heard. He was excused.

Linthicum stood up: "Your Honor, that concludes the preliminaries of why we have no witnesses. We respectfully request that the transcript of the original trial be used in their place."

"How could the transcript provide all the information," Menchine asked him, "when the witnesses are not here and the State has conceded conflicts in the girl's testimony? If we used the transcript as evidence, wouldn't that serve to perpetuate the falsity of the first trial?"

"We can't impeach the evidence," said Forer (and later Linthicum concurred), "because to do that you have to lay the grounds and without witnesses, that is impossible . . . nor could we cross-examine."

Forer had labeled the transcript "tainted testimony." Menchine had no intention of taking sides on that issue. "The Court makes no finding that there is the slightest taint on the testimony, or that there was any wrongdoing on the part of the State. But the transcript cannot be accepted for the reason that it would prevent the defense from attempting to show that it was tainted."

Then he began a speech which lasted for twenty minutes and cited precedent after precedent, at length concluding with "the transcript may not be introduced." It was then Linthicum's turn.

"We know we can never get the female witness," he said, "and as to the male witness, we're not convinced it's impossible, but we're not prepared to make the lengthy attempt again. In view of all these problems, I have no alternative but to move that the case be nolle prossed."

Joe Forer was on his feet at once. "Object," he said. "Object. My clients demand a trial." ("I did that for the record," he explained later. "In common law, if a nolle pross motion is made without the consent of a defendant, once a trial has begun, the nolle pross amounts to an acquittal.")

His objection was overruled.

"You are discharged," said Menchine to the Giles, and the courtroom emptied. In the sunshine outside, reporters and photographers focused on the Giles, the attorneys, Mrs. Ross, and Harold Knapp.

There was relief but no jubilation this time. "Do you remember," Barbara Knapp asked Mrs. Ross, "that we used to wonder how it would end? Whether it would be with a bang or a whimper? Well, you can't call nolle prossing a bang, exactly. But at least they're free."

XXIII

Getting Joe Johnson out of prison was another matter. From the moment Forer and Witt made their first move in that direction after the Giles were freed (a petition to have his conviction set aside), it became clear that the legal establishment had closed its ranks and was going to maintain a united front against any outside pressure.

The State had confessed error once in this case, but it seemed to have no intention, nor see any reason, for doing so again. They had "carefully studied" the transcript of Joe Johnson's trial in 1962, said Attorney General Burch and William Linthicum. In it they had found "no error" such as they had in the police testimony in the Giles trial. Therefore they would oppose either the setting aside of Johnson's conviction or a new trial for him.

On the other hand, they would be glad to help him in an appeal to the Governor for pardon, they said, and often repeated. (Pardon by the executive would, of course, absolve the judiciary from responsibility.)

"The Johnson case," commented Joe Forer, "is as full of holes as the Giles case. We have no intention of applying for a pardon."

Joe's post-conviction hearing began in Anne Arundel County, in Annapolis, on November 20, bringing him out of the penitentiary for the first time since he had been placed on its

Death Row in 1962. He had matured in those years, and had
lost the "scared rabbit look" which had once seemed so marked
to Mrs. Ross. Now, he sat stoically beside Forer and Witt.

The judge that Monday was E. Mackall Childs, small-nosed,
small-faced, and so patently hostile to Joe Forer and the burden
of his argument that the committee felt from the start that
there was little hope he would see any legal "holes" in Johnson's case. It was hard, however, to know whether he heard or
saw anything: he sat with his head bent, continually writing—
was he making notes?—and on the few occasions he spoke or
asked a question, he never lifted his head, so that his words
were difficult to hear.

Linthicum, earnest and youthful as always, took the line
that the defense by the time of Joe Johnson's trial knew far
more than the prosecution did: a committee had hired a private
detective to look into Stella's history; and Johnson's court-
appointed lawyer, Crawford, had attended the Giles trial, and
thus had observed a kind of dress rehearsal of Joe's trial a year
later. And lastly, he said, no such arguments mattered anyway.
In a post-conviction hearing all that mattered was whether
there had been legal defects in the original trial, and as far as
he was concerned, there had been none. He repeated that he
would gladly urge the defense to appeal for a pardon.

Forer put stacks of written material in evidence and called
a variety of witnesses in the course of the two-day hearing. But
his key witness, as all recognized, was Mrs. Olson, whom—
with her son Richard Johnson—the committee had again flown
in from the West. Whether she was as frightened this time
as she had been on the day the State confessed error, no one
could guess. Dressed in black, with a strand of pearls, she appeared composed as she told the story of Stella's telephone call,
and how she, Mrs. Olson, had called Kardy the next day from
her office—probably close to 2:00, as she testified later—only
to be told by him that the case was finished and that he had

all the evidence he needed. She had called Kardy on the twenty-seventh, being sure of the date because she had got his name from a newspaper account of the trial, which had finished the day before. (The newspaper was put in evidence.)

The date was crucial to the "credibility" of Leonard Kardy, since it would have fallen within Maryland's then Three-Day Rule on the acceptance of new evidence. "Why didn't you call the defense lawyers, Crawford and Heeney?" asked Linthicum on cross-examination.

"Because I thought it was the duty of the State's Attorney to accept evidence," she answered.

She testified in the morning. In the afternoon Leonard Kardy was put on the stand, and in his gray silk suit was low-keyed and extremely polite to Forer. The upshot of his answers was that he had made no attempt to investigate either Stella or William; he had "relied totally on the investigation of Lieutenant Whelan."

Then Linthicum took him on for cross-examination, trying to undermine Mrs. Olson's testimony:

Q. Now, at the conclusion of the trial, where did you go then?

A. I believe I was staying at the Maryland Inn at that time and I believe after the jury came back that I went back to the Maryland Inn and I believe I stayed the night.

Q. And when did you return to Montgomery County?

A. To the best of my recollection, knowledge, information and belief, I came back to Montgomery County the next day which would be September 27, 1962 with Mr. Crawford and Mr. Heeney [the two lawyers defending Joe Johnson]. I did not have my car here. They drove me to my home . . . and I believe we arrived . . . 2:00–3:00 in the afternoon of the 27th.

Q. Did you return to the State's Attorney's office that day?

A. To the best of my knowledge, information and belief and reconstructing from the records and also from dis-

cussions with Mr. Heeney and Mr. Crawford, I did not
return to my office that day.

As the story was pieced together from the testimony of
Kardy, Crawford, and Heeney, it seemed that Kardy had been
driven to Annapolis—not much more than an hour's drive
from Rockville—by his assistant Cromwell, who had returned
the next day, immediately after the trial was finished, about
2:30 in the afternoon. Kardy and the defense lawyers, however, had stayed in Annapolis until some time the following
day. Why, without having any business in Annapolis that next
morning, had the lawyers remained? Kardy did not know, but
he assumed "they were tired after a strenuous case." They had
stayed at the Maryland Inn, gone together for a late dinner at
the Red Coach, which no longer existed, and had not started
the drive back until about noon the next day—the twenty-
seventh—although Kardy thought they started later. Kardy
had been deposited at his home first; the other two had paused
for Heeney to show Crawford around his small farm, drop
him at his house, and then go on into Rockville to his office.
There, Heeney's records showed, he had kept a 2:45 appointment, although all his morning appointments had been can-
celed. Neither of the other two kept daily office records. Therefore, there was no way to prove or disprove Kardy's statement
that he had not been in his office and could not have received
Mrs. Olson's call.

Why had Kardy not told Linthicum about this before, when
—as Linthicum had told him previously—he and Kardy had
discussed the matter of Mrs. Olson's affidavit? Because, Kardy
answered Forer, he had completely forgotten the episode until
Crawford and Heeney had refreshed his recollection at lunch
today.

    Q.   Well, when you say they refreshed your recollection,
did they refresh your recollection or did you just accept
their version as being accurate?

A.   No, sir, they refreshed my recollection . . . .

Q.   Well, did they refresh your recollection that after they
      dropped you at your home you did not go back to the
      office?

A.   No, refreshing my recollection I stayed at home because
      it was later in the afternoon. I didn't go to my office,
      Mr. Forer.

They had refreshed his memory correctly on where he had
been the night of September 26. The hotel register for the year
1962 had gone into storage, but was dug out and produced for
the second morning of the hearing when Mr. Atkinson—portly,
middle-aged—took the stand to be questioned by Linthicum.

A.   I am innkeeper, or manager, whichever you prefer, of
      the Maryland Inn, here on Church Circle in Annapolis.

Q.   . . . Mr. Atkinson, I show you a piece of paper and ask
      you if you can tell the Court what that is.

A.   That is the record of a payment back in September 27,
      1962 of a suite, occupied by "Mr. Kardy and One."

The bill also showed Kardy as having paid $2.25 plus a fifty-
cent tip on the twenty-seventh for what the Court decided,
with Atkinson's concurrence, must have been breakfast on that
day.

("What really revolts me," said one committee member later,
"is the picture I get: Kardy, who'd just got a successful conviction he knew would mean the death sentence; the two defense
lawyers who'd failed to prevent that conviction—all three of
them staying over to join in a late dinner, being 'tired after a
strenuous case' and obviously not being up to driving back till
noon the next day.")

Judge Childs heard oral arguments two months later. Shortly
before twelve noon, when both Forer and Linthicum had finished, he said: "I am prepared to give my decision now. However, I think it preferable to wait until after a luncheon recess.

We will reconvene at one thirty. What I shall then say may displease some in this room; therefore, there will be no demonstration of any kind, nor will anyone be permitted to enter or leave while I am speaking."

On the dot of 1:30 guards stationed themselves on the inside of the courtroom doors and thereafter no latecomer was permitted to enter. It took Judge Childs thirty-five minutes to read a speech necessarily written before he heard the oral arguments that morning. What he said followed—sometimes even to the word—Linthicum's previous argument. Each of Forer's points he discounted. As to "this amazing information" Mrs. Olson said she had relayed to Mr. Kardy, he spoke at some length, saying, in part:

> This Court has been furnished with no legal authority whatsoever by either the Petitioner or the State on the proposition that exculpatory evidence obtained by the State after the trial must be divulged to the person convicted. The Court has likewise been unable to find precedent for this novel proposition . . . .
>
> . . . The Court is not prepared to say that this was information which Kardy was required to relay to the defense. However, to place such speculation at an end, this Court finds that the conversation which was alleged by Petitioners to have taken place between Mrs. Olson and Mr. Kardy did not, in fact, take place . . . .

And at another point he said that despite the "hydroesque" ruling of the Supreme Court, he could find no basis for awarding Joe Johnson a new trial.

Joe Johnson continued to sit stoically, with no expression on his face whatsoever, through Childs' speech. He remained expressionless afterward as the very large, heavy-set prison guard handcuffed him and led him out. The waiting van was a new type, more secure than previous ones, with both horizontal and vertical iron bars. Joe got in first, the guard followed, and then the driver clanged shut the double doors on the back and fastened across the two bars.

Others were not stoic. Joe's father was weeping and so were several of the committee. Harold Knapp, unable to bear the scene they had all just witnessed, leaped into the front of the van and called to the guard inside, "Be kind to him."

"It is an insult to intelligence" editorialized the *Post* (January 25, 1968),

> and to the common sense of justice that Joseph Johnson should remain in prison under a life sentence, while the Giles brothers are at liberty with the charges against them dismissed . . . . The State, having wrongly convicted these three young men . . . has now acted . . . to compound its guilt by meanly and stubbornly insisting that it will not free Johnson until it is forced to do so . . . .

One thing more needs to be said:

> In rejecting the petition for a new trial put forward by counsel for Johnson, Judge E. Mackall Childs of Anne Arundel Circuit Court displayed a combination of petulance and prejudice. He appears to consider it some sort of *lèse majesté* for the Supreme Court of the United States to upset a conviction obtained in a state court. That sort of callous indifference to justice is precisely what makes Supreme Court intervention necessary. State's Attorney William Linthicum displayed an equal indifference.

The committee met the evening after Joe had been returned to the penitentiary.

"Well, they won," said Forer. "I know we can win eventually, perhaps even on appeal. But that might take another six years and we just can't do that to Joe. I followed him over to the penitentiary today. He's in terrible shape; he wants no more of the courts, and I can't blame him. So we have to plea for pardon. It's a shame that the wrong done in the judicial system was not righted in the judicial system, but there it is."

The petition for pardon was ready within a week, and the legal establishment—Leonard Kardy, William Linthicum, Attorney General Burch, the original defense lawyer Crawford—magnanimously joined the numbers of those writing or wiring the Governor on Joe's behalf. And when Frances Ross, Joe Forer, and Hal Witt sat at lunch in Annapolis, waiting to present the petition to Governor Agnew, Judge E. Mackall Childs, who had condemned Joe Johnson to life imprisonment, paused at their table to wish them luck!

On the tenth of February, 1968, Governor Agnew gave Joe full and complete pardon, which totally cleared his record. As soon as possible thereafter, the committee held a large public meeting. Frances Ross spoke only to introduce the treasurer and her report of collections over six and a half years. Joe Johnson, in a new dark suit, said a few words of thanks, and was followed by James Giles—now at the end of his first week as a freshman in college; last came John, somehow overcoming his crippling shyness to add his thanks.

But it was really Joe Forer's evening. He stood facing an audience which more often had seen only his back in the courtroom, and spoke without notes, sketching first the history of Joe Johnson's case and explaining why he and Hat Witt had handled it as they had. Then he changed his subject: "The question arises whether we have accomplished anything. Quite obviously we have; we rescued three young men; we *did* it. There's no question about that. When I say we, I mean us and the committee and the people who backed us. We got them out. It wasn't easy. It took several years and cost a lot of money and a tremendous amount of effort. When I think of the amount of time Frances Ross spent, just on the telephone . . . ! Well, that much we have accomplished.

"Have we accomplished anything else? First, has this case resulted or is it likely to result in some general improvement in the administration of justice? I think it will have an effect, but I don't think we can overestimate that effect. It may be . . . that when the State has evidence of innocence it won't conceal it, but will reveal it.

"Then, I think that for a while, here in Maryland, and in a certain location, at least, the police may be a little hesitant as to the kind of testimony they give. Even more important it might be—although I kind of doubt it—that they will conduct generally unbiased investigations, instead of the kind they did here.

"Then, I think the case has had a good influence on our own thinking, the thinking of the people who have worked on it and got some knowledge of it. I'm a lawyer and I've been a lawyer for many years . . . . I've evolved a kind of cynicism about our administration of justice, because I don't think it lives up to its protestation.

"And yet I think that most of the people on the Giles-Johnson Defense Committee, at the beginning, shared the kind of American view that our courts are infallible . . . somehow they think they can take some politician and put him on the bench and he'll get rid of all his prejudices, or turn into a genius, no matter how stupid he was before.

"Of course, it's logical for people to feel that way; it makes them feel more comfortable to let the courts administer justice and handle life and death, and if people had to assume responsibility, it might be uncomfortable. So it's easier to say, 'Oh well, they'll settle it.' And that's one of the reasons why we don't have a better system for the administration of more justice.

"And I must say the members of the judicial establishment tend to perpetuate this myth as, for example, the judge who very seriously criticized Mrs. Ross. 'How dare you question our

judicial system in the Giles-Johnson case? Don't you know'—
well, at least this was the gist of his complaint—'that things
will right themselves and the judiciary will take care of things?'

"Well, I think it's good for people to know there are these
defects and fallacies in our judicial system. It's good for them
to know because—well, all I can say is that if everything had
been left to the judicial system, these three young men would
not be with us tonight."